THE INDEPENDENT FILMMAKER'S GUIDE

THE INDEPENDENT FILMMAKER'S GUIDE

Make Your Feature Film for $2000

GLENN BERGGOETZ

AN IMPRINT OF HAL LEONARD CORPORATION

Published in 2012 by Limelight Editions
An Imprint of Hal Leonard Corporation
7777 West Bluemound Road
Milwaukee, WI 53213

Trade Book Division Editorial Offices
33 Plymouth St., Montclair, NJ 07042

Printed in the United States of America

Book design by Mark Lerner

Library of Congress Cataloging-in-Publication Data

Berggoetz, Glenn.
 The independent filmmaker's guide : make your feature film for $2000 / Glenn Berggoetz.
     p. cm.
 Includes index.
 ISBN 978-0-87910-423-8 (pbk.)
 1. Motion pictures--Production and direction. 2. Low budget films. I. Title.
 PN1995.9.P7B365 2012
 791.43'0232--dc23
                        2012025304

www.limelighteditions.com

To Diane Henry—Thank you for being you

Contents

THE INDEPENDENT FILMMAKER'S GUIDE

Introduction

I've heard it and read it dozens of times—it takes tens of thousands of dollars and years of hard work to make a feature film. Both claims are completely not true, and I'm living proof of that. While you certainly can spend your life savings and max out every credit card you can get your hands on, and spend three, four, or even five years making your film, you can also spend $1100 and four months making a feature film, as I did when I made *The Worst Movie EVER!*

The film world is constantly changing. Fifteen years ago, when making a film meant buying and developing copious amounts of actual film, filmmakers were pretty much left with no alternative but to spend an absolute minimum of $20,000 to make a feature. But with the advent of digital film and digital cameras, and with the ability to now record your film almost directly into a computer, those days are gone. No longer must a filmmaker invest a small fortune into film alone.

But what about paying a cast and crew? That can come a lot cheaper than you think. There are so many hungry actors, actresses, camera people, and sound people out there who will do just about anything to work on a film that it's quite easy to find competent, sometimes exceedingly talented, people to work on your films for gas money and some free food.

I have made many films over the last five years, some shorts, but mostly features. My feature films *Therapissed*, *Separate Checks*, and *Evil Intent* quickly landed distribution deals. My feature film *To Die is Hard* won a Golden Ace Award and received a theatrical release. My feature film *The Worst Movie EVER!* also got a theatrical release, both in the United States and in Europe, and has a worldwide distribution deal. How much did it cost me to make these five feature films? Seventy-seven hundred dollars. Total. That's right, $7700, for an average of $1540 per film. Entertaining films can be made on a shoestring budget.

Did I go to film school? No. All I really wanted to be was a scriptwriter. At 38 years old, I had spent nearly a decade writing scripts on the side, and eventually I had nine completed feature film scripts. Could I get anyone in Hollywood to take a look at them? No.

So one day, while living in Denver, Colorado, I spoke with a guy who used to work in Hollywood and told him about my scripts. He suggested that the best way to break into Hollywood would be to make my own films, and that if I did it well, I'd get noticed.

From there I read a couple of books on filmmaking and directing. It was a bit overwhelming. The books on filmmaking made making a film seem like a Herculean task, that to make a film was a talent reserved for the gods, that mere mortals shouldn't even deign to undertake such an endeavor. But such was my mania to make a film that I pressed on.

I decided to start by making a short film. The film was titled *Bad Movies, Good Showers, and Civil Engineers*. It was a simple film that followed the conversations simultaneously taking place at four tables in a restaurant. I figured it would be wise to do something simple as I learned the process.

One of the first obstacles I faced was that the script was 22 pages long, but over and over in the books I read, I came across the thought that to shoot even five pages of script in a single day was quite remarkable, and I planned to shoot the entire film in one day. A few people told me I was biting off more than I could chew, but I thought, "How difficult can it be to film people talking?" So I pressed on.

The day of the shoot arrived, and we arrived on set at 7 a.m. that day. Things went smoothly as I frequently let the more veteran cast and crew members do their thing. The shooting went quickly. And I began to notice some things. I noticed that there was plenty of natural light flooding the set, and that we didn't really need a lighting technician—all we needed was maybe one or two lamps or reading lights to fill in some shadows. (Shadows in a scene are typically considered taboo to many filmmakers, camera people, and lighting technicians because they are seen as being amateurish when they appear in a film, but who cares about shadows? Life is filled with shadows!) I noticed we didn't really need a sound guy with lots of elaborate equipment, that all we really needed was anyone who could hold a boom microphone. I realized I didn't need a director of photography and two additional camera people, that we could have gotten by with the DP working a camera and one other cameraperson. I realized I didn't need to put so much time and money into making sure there was plenty of food to eat, because most cast members were only on set for a little while, and most crew members are happy with cookies and potato chips (the healthy foods I brought to the set went almost completely untouched). And I realized that the shoot was flying by—we shot all 22 pages by 4 p.m.

I also quickly realized that much of the information I had read in books on filmmaking was useless (you don't need to know what a gaffer, second assistant director, and line producer do), that the books could have been whittled down from 400 and 500 pages to about 50-100 pages. So often filmmakers get caught up in so much useless minutiae in shooting their film that the film suffers, the shoot drags on, the cast and crew gets cranky, and the bank account dwindles. None of this is necessary.

Over the course of the next six months I made two more short films to familiarize myself with the filmmaking process. All the while I was working on feature scripts that would be easy to shoot, and seven months after making my first short film, I embarked on shooting my first feature film.

While on the topic of short films, let me point out now that short films are primarily masturbatory exercises. For the most part, they're only good for learning how to make feature films. In very, very rare instances, a short film might be so good as to end up being a filmmaker's big break, but the other 99.99% of the time, there are so many people making so many short films and showing them in so many film festivals where there is not one person in attendance who can do anything to make or break your career that the making of the short film is nothing more than an opportunity to practice your craft a bit. Short films aren't going to get a DVD release, they're not going to be shown in theaters (with very rare exceptions), they're not going to get shown by a television network (again, with very rare exceptions), and you're not going to be able to sell them in the foreign markets, so don't waste your time making short films, make features.

When pointing out these issues regarding the making of short films to other filmmakers, one of the responses I often get is that the big benefit to making short films is that good ones get accepted into film festivals, so you can attend the festivals and network with other filmmakers. While in principle this sounds good, keep in mind who you will be networking with—people exactly like you! You're going to meet a whole bunch of people who are also trying to get distribution deals and money to make their future films. It's a bit like unemployed people networking with other unemployed people. Sure, you might have a good time and meet some interesting people, but everyone you meet is also unemployed and looking for a job, and no one that you meet will be in a position to offer you a job. While I have met plenty of great people at film festivals, including some who have become friends and given me some sage advice and a little help over the years with my feature films, the argument that making short films is a good way to network at film festivals is a tenuous argument at best.

Keep in mind that your feature films don't have to be big productions. The best example I can give of this is my comedic feature film *Separate Checks*. I specifically wrote the film so that it would be simple to shoot by limiting the cast to three people—Libby Baker, Greg Nemer, and me. I limited the locations to two—my apartment and the sidewalk around the corner from my apartment—so we didn't have to worry about lugging equipment around from location to location. And I limited the number of crew members by keeping all scenes in the film as day scenes (no need for a lighting technician) and by holding the boom myself, so the entire crew consisted of me and the director of photography/editor, Nick Falls. That meant the entire cast and crew consisted of four people.

The film is simple—it's basically two people talking for eighty minutes, trying to figure out where their relationship and their lives are going. Yes, there isn't a huge market for films like that, as many film fans like lots of explosions and excitement, but there are many upsides in making such a film. First off, it only cost $800 to make. Second, if you get a fantastic performance from one of your cast members (and I got great performances from both Libby and Greg), the film could be sellable based on that alone. Third, if the writing is good enough it may draw some attention that opens up other doors for you. And fourth, should Libby or Greg make it big (and Libby has been a co-star on the Emmy Award–winning TV show *Modern Family* and has appeared on other sitcoms, so she's well on her way), there will certainly be a market for the film as their fans want to see them in other projects. Is *Separate Checks* the next *Citizen Kane* or *Caddyshack*? No. But it is a funny, entertaining film that was made for less than a thousand dollars that could open up some doors for us.

At this point, let me set the record straight for how my film *The Worst Movie EVER!* set the all-time box office record for the worst opening weekend and the worst opening week in box office history when it brought in just $11 its first weekend and week in release. There has been a lot of discussion on Internet websites that the whole thing was a publicity stunt orchestrated from the beginning to set this record. Those kinds of discussions could not be farther from the truth.

What happened was that a theater in Los Angeles emailed me on a Sunday and said they wanted to show *The Worst Movie EVER!* on the upcoming Friday and Saturday nights as a midnight movie. When I read the email late on Sunday, I was thrilled. While the film had already been booked into a theater in Virginia for a few weeks down the road, this screening would now be the theatrical premiere for the film, and the premiere would be in LA. The problem was that I was in Indiana at the time I received the email, and the next day I would be traveling to Denver, so it wouldn't be until Tuesday that I would be able to really begin to let people know about the screening.

On Tuesday I began to email the few people I knew in LA about the screening and post notices on Facebook, but there really wasn't any time to do any advertising for the film. I wasn't too upset by this, though, as I figured that since the film was screening in LA, fifty or a hundred people would see the marquee each night and stroll into the theater out of curiosity's sake to watch the film. It didn't turn out that way.

It turned out that the theater complex never put the film up on the marquee and simply showed *The Worst Movie EVER!* in one of their side theaters while other films were being shown at midnight in their main theaters. Because of the lack of advertising and the lack of marquee publicity, and factoring in that of the few people I knew in LA, none of them were able to attend either of the screenings, just one person total showed up for the two nights and paid $11 to see the film.

When I received the box office numbers the following Monday, I was devastated. I didn't want to tell anyone about the debacle, but I had promised my contact at Boxofficemojo.com, Ray Subers, that I would get him the box office numbers when I had them. I emailed him the numbers that Monday, and Ray emailed me right back and asked if there was a typo. I said no, and Ray posted the numbers on Boxofficemojo.

I assumed the matter was dead at this point and no one else would ever know of our horrendous showing, only to find out that Stu VanAirsdale, who runs the film and film industry website Movieline.com, noticed our $11 total on Boxofficemojo and ran an article on Tuesday about the new record we had just set. He also posted the trailer of *The Worst Movie EVER!* with the article. By the next day, the film was an Internet sensation, and since then we've gotten the film into numerous theaters and landed a worldwide distribution deal.

Was this whole thing orchestrated? Not in the least. Were we the beneficiaries of pure, dumb luck? Absolutely.

Enough about that. Now let's get into the nuts and bolts of how you can go about making a feature film for less than $2000. Maybe a whole lot less than $2000.

CHAPTER 1

The Script

The single most important thing to making a good movie is to have a good script. If there is one aspect of the filmmaking process that needs to be done as perfectly as possible, it's making sure you have a good script to work with. Unfortunately, many aspiring filmmakers think this means they need to spend a year or two writing their script and revising it over and over again. This is absolutely not the case.

I realize I'm different from most filmmakers in this regard since I love the writing process, but for me, even for a feature-length script, I typically spend a few days jotting down ideas, spend one to two weeks writing the first draft, and then take another week or two to tighten it up. We're not writing *War and Peace* here.

Think of it this way. A feature film script is usually around 15,000 words or so in length. This is equivalent in length to a short novella. Heck, it can almost be classified as a long short story, and I'm guessing not many of us would think it wise to spend a year or two working on one short story when we see Stephen King releasing multiple tomes every year.

I know this year-long process is the mindset of many aspiring filmmakers because no more than a month ago (and I've heard it often during the Q&A sessions of my speaking engagements), a guy approached me and told me he wanted to make a film, which would be his first. He told me he had an idea for a script and was ready to begin writing it. He then proceeded to say, "Now, I need to set aside a year or so for writing this script, don't I?" No! No, you don't. Dive into the writing process with vigor. You will probably find that when you move quickly on your script, ideas will spring forth, ideas that aren't in your notes that will add depth to your script. Don't discount the power of the creative juices that are flowing. I can't count the number of times I've been working feverishly on a script and suddenly said out loud "Oh, my gosh!" as something unexpected came to mind to include in the script. It might have been a plot twist, a new character, a funny line, or whatever, but I'm guessing that 90% or more of those ideas would never have occurred to me had I been taking the approach that two or three times a week I would sit down and see if I could get a single page written (which is about the pace you would have to go at if you planned to take a year to write your script).

There is also no point in getting into the mindset that only a couple of pages a day can be written. When the ideas have formed for a script, get them down on paper or in your computer. When I had the idea for the film *Evil Intent*, I jotted down notes for the script for two days, sat down at the computer to begin writing the script on a Friday afternoon, and finished the first draft on Monday morning. Was the script perfect? No, it certainly needed revising. But in less than a week's time I went from the conception of the film to a completed script, and then the filmmaking process could begin.

Pretty much the same can be said for my films *To Die is Hard* and *The Worst Movie EVER!* With *To Die is Hard*, my good friend and frequent film collaborator Alan Dague-Greene was in the process of downloading some footage for me that we had shot for our sketch comedy TV show *Driving With Our Eyes Shut*. In one of the sketches, I played a macho action hero who acts belligerent and tough as he opens fire on an unknown assailant as a mass of cowering people huddle behind a table next to him. Alan thought the scene was hilarious and said I should write an entire script around this premise. I liked the idea, so I made some notes over the next few days over what I wanted to have happen in the film and then began writing. A week later the script was done.

With *The Worst Movie EVER!* I had noticed for quite a while that in way too many films there are god-awful characters, dialogue, effects, etc., that frequently pop up. Every now and then when I would see something like this in a film, I'd say to myself, "Gosh, that scene/character/ dialogue would fit perfectly in a film titled *The Worst Movie Ever*." Eventually I began to realize that there are so many examples of this awfulness that I could make an entire film out of awful characters, plots, and dialogue, so I made some notes, started writing, and six days later the first draft of the script was completed.

This doesn't mean the script is finished when the first draft is completed. Far from it. But the rewriting process does not have to take a year or more. In my case I'm fortunate to work with Alan, who has an incredible sense of humor and a sense for what works on screen and what doesn't. Alan is the only person I really take constructive feedback from, and I suggest you do the same—limit yourself in the number of people you allow to comment on your script. It's quite easy for aspiring filmmakers to not trust their own judgment and get five or ten people to read their script, and then try to incorporate the suggestions of all these people into their rewrite. This is a recipe for disaster. The old cliché that too many cooks spoil the broth is absolutely in effect when it comes to writing a good script. Scripts that get the input of too many people run the risk of being directionless as each person commenting on the script tends to want to take the script in a little different direction than everyone else (whether it's with the plot, characterization, dialogue, etc.), and you end up with an awful mess of a script. Trust yourself, trust your vision. After all, you're making a film, and it's going to be your name attached to the film. Don't let your name be attached to something that isn't your dream, that isn't your vision.

As you do your rewrite, be open to changes. I've found that I typically end up adding in more content as I do a rewrite. I've also found that as I go through a draft of the script, sometimes what seemed funny or interesting to me at the time I was writing the first draft just doesn't work very well when I've had a chance to sit down and read the script straight through. Nothing is sacred in a script. If a line or a scene or a character needs to go, get rid of it. If you need to add dialogue to a scene, do it. If you need to add in a scene to smooth out a transition, do it. Always keep in mind that the ultimate goal is to have a great script, and that often means cutting things you thought were pure gold in the first draft, or making a drastic change with a scene or a character.

Finally, I have found it conducive to get into a specific writing habit when writing and revising my scripts. For me, I'm an early riser, and I typically go for a walk around five in the morning or so and think over ideas for what I want to do with the script. As soon as my walk is completed, I begin to write, and I frequently write straight through the morning. Sometime between 11 a.m. and 1 p.m. I usually knock off for the day, and then the next day I start the process all over again. This works for me; however, if you're not a morning person, find a few hours each afternoon to work on your script, or if you're a night person, begin writing at 8 p.m. and write until midnight. Whatever your schedule, find one that works for you and stick to it—it'll get you on your path to getting your script completed in a reasonable amount of time and allow you get on with the shooting of your film.

Keep It Simple

When making a low-budget film, always keep in mind that you need to keep your script as simple as possible. What do I mean by that? Quite simply, limiting the number of characters in the film and limiting the number of locations in the film. You're making a film for less than $2000—no one expects you to make another *Gone with the Wind* or *Apocalypse Now* with that kind of money. You're making a film that you hope will get your foot into the film industry door so you can eventually make a living by making films, and to do that, with your micro budget, you need to keep things simple.

When it comes to the cast of the film, the fewer cast members the better. With *Evil Intent*, there are only five people in the entire film. With *Separate Checks* there are only three people in the film. Can this make your film look low budget?

Of course it can. But your film is low budget, and you can make an interesting, engaging film with just a handful of characters. In some of my other films we used bigger casts, sometimes as many as fifteen people. But keep a few things in mind as your cast begins to grow.

First off, the more cast members you have, the more money it's going to cost you to make your film. It costs money to get actors and actresses to work on your film, and while you're not going to be giving them much money to be in your film, you should always give them at least gas money, and, if possible, $50 to $100 each for their time and efforts. Second, more cast members means more money spent on food for the shoot (though this doesn't have to be that much, as I'll explain later). And third, more cast members means more chances for having someone show up late or even completely miss a shooting day, which can completely screw up the shooting schedule. Believe you me, making sure you have four people on set at any given time is a heck of a lot easier and less stressful than trying to make sure you have 15 people all on set at the same time.

So rule one in writing your script is to limit the number of cast members. Those ideas you have for a script that has 40 cast members? Save that for when you get a few million dollars to make a film.

The second rule for your script is to limit the number of locations. With *Evil Intent*, we shot nearly the entire film in one house, simply moving from room to room to change things up a bit. The only other location we used was my apartment, for the scenes in the psychologist's office. With our feature film *Therapissed* we used the same house we shot *Evil Intent* in and my same apartment for every scene. With *To Die is Hard* we used one apartment and one college campus building. With *The Worst Movie EVER!* we used two houses and my apartment. So much time is wasted when moving from one location to another that it tremendously slows down the shoot, and when you're paying people only $50 or so to be in your movie, you better do everything you possibly can to make the shoot go quickly and smoothly so each person only has to be on set for one or two days.

Another nice thing about limiting your locations to houses is that you will pretty much always be able to find a cast or crew member who is willing to let you shoot at their house for free, which is not only convenient, but it can save you hundreds of dollars compared to renting a business or public space for a day or two. The cast or crew member loves this because they then don't have to go anywhere to be in the film, and you love it because then you get to use a location for free, which fits nicely into your small budget.

If you have to use locations other than houses and apartments for your film (or just want to use other locations to spice up your film), check with friends and cast and crew members to see if any of them have access to a location you can use in your film that is free and convenient. A great example of this is an office, or even an office building, that a friend might work in. It is sometimes easy to get into an office or an office building on a Saturday or Sunday to shoot a few scenes there, and often the person getting you into this location doesn't even have to tell their boss or security that you will be filming there, which means you'll be using the location for free. When you get the okay from someone to use a location like this, go ahead and incorporate that location into your script.

Another matter to keep in mind with your script is to keep it as short as you can while making sure your film is at least 70 minutes in length (the typical cut-off point for your film to be considered a feature film and to have a chance to get into theaters). Even better, make sure your film ends up 80–85 minutes in length, which will make it even easier to find a buyer for your film, as there is no doubt that a film of 80 minutes or more in length falls into the feature film category. If you end up with a film that's 66 minutes in length, you basically have a worthless film, for even though it might be engaging, entertaining, funny, or wonderfully dramatic, no theater is going to run a film of this length, and television networks don't have a time slot for films of this length.

To make sure your film ends up somewhere within these parameters, you're looking at a script of approximately 90–95 pages in length. If you find your script creeping up to 100–120 pages in length, it's probably getting too long, unless your script is almost nothing but dialogue, in which case you may need 110 pages of script to end up with an 80-minute movie. Keep in mind that since many small-budget films are more dialogue-driven than Hollywood productions, and that dialogue on the printed page moves more quickly than explanation of action on a page, your script probably won't fit into the standard mold of one page of script equaling one minute of film. So your script will need to be around 90–100 pages in length to make sure your film ends up at least 80 minutes long.

If you don't know how to format your script, simply hop onto the Internet, where you'll be able to quickly find multiple examples of how you can properly format your script.

Finally, since you only have a small budget, don't include any explosions or major special effects in your script. Save these things for when you have $20 million at your disposal.

What Not to Do

Here's an example of what not to do when trying to make your first feature film, and I use this example from someone who wanted to make a short film.

A really talented guy I know wanted to make a really cool short film. I read the script, which was six pages long. The script, while engaging, was quite intricate, not from a casting point of view (there were only four characters), but from a location point of view. One of the scenes in the script required an elevated railroad trestle. By scouring the Internet, this guy was able to find the perfect trestle for his film—over a thousand miles away! Not very practical for making a low-budget film. On top of that, to get a particular shot he wanted, he would need to rent a helicopter. Now, typically, you would think that making a little five-minute short film would be a simple endeavor, but between having to take a cast and crew a thousand miles away, put them up in hotels, feed them, and rent a helicopter, you're looking at a major expenditure of both time and money. Has this film been made? No. Will it ever get made? Probably not.

Also keep in mind that in making a small-budget film, you may have plenty of scenes that are heavily dialogue-driven. This is frequently a necessity in keeping your locations and costs down, and there is absolutely no shame in having lots of dialogue in your film (it's worked out pretty well for Woody Allen), though it does put a heavy emphasis on making sure your script is solid.

When I was preparing to make my first film, a 19-minute short titled *Bad Movies, Good Showers, and Civil Engineers*, I posted an ad on an Internet site looking for cast and crew members. I received a lot of responses (there are always hundreds of people out there looking to work on films), and one of the guys who contacted me was interested in being the director of photography for the film, so I emailed him the script. I soon heard back from him in the form of a lengthy and angry email. In this email the guy told me that he was fed up with all these small-budget independent films and scripts that were not much more than people sitting around and talking (*Bad Movies, Good Showers, and Civil Engineers* is nothing but people sitting around and talking). He wanted to see scripts with action in them, where something happened besides talking. Well, you know what? To make a film with a small budget, it's often imperative to have a dialogue-driven script. And to that guy who sent me that angry email: if you're so fed up with those kinds of films, why don't you write your own scripts and make your own films?

There is one other issue that needs to be addressed with the script, and that concerns the value of the script when it comes to directing your film. I have found that the better my script is, the less directing I have to do. Actors and actresses are talented people, and if you give them good material to work with, more often than not, they'll do good things with that material without you having to say much once the shoot gets going. So make the effort to make sure you have a good script, and your duties as a director will largely take care of themselves.

Genres

So what kind of script should you write? Comedy? Drama? Horror? Action? To maximize your chances of eventually getting a distribution deal, your best bet is to stay away from dramas and go with either a comedy or a horror script. Even an action film will be an easier sell than a drama script. Here's why.

Most filmmakers want to make dramas because most people who are in the film industry or who simply like films think that the way for a filmmaker to establish him- or herself as a great filmmaker is to make a powerful, riveting drama. While this might be so, because so many people want to make this kind of film, there are thousands of competently made independent dramas that you'll have to compete with. In addition, since dramas are so prevalent, most buyers won't even look at a drama unless it has at least one well-known name appearing in it. Since you're making your film on a shoestring budget, your odds of landing even a B-list figure for your film are slim.

Good comedies, on the other hand, aren't so easy to make. Let's face it, most indie comedies aren't very funny. But when a comedy is well made and is funny, whether it has a known name in the film or not, people will still watch it. So if you're capable of making a good comedy film, make that film instead of a drama because it has a better chance of finding a deal.

Horror films are also a better way for getting your foot in the door. Millions of horror fans will watch just about any horror film because, if it's well made and scary, it works as a horror film. Conversely, if it's poorly made, a horror film can often work as a comedy. And certainly with horror films, there's no requirement to have a big name attached to the film.

With action films, your small budget will limit the kind of action you can put in your film (you probably won't be able to afford any chase scenes, car crash scenes, explosions, etc.), but there's definitely a fan base of people who like to watch fighting and other forms of action in films. So even with an unknown cast, your well-made action film will have a chance of getting picked up by someone.

There is one interesting note to consider when deciding on the genre of the script you're going to write. A few years ago a Hollywood insider made a survey of 20 Hollywood studio executives. Among the questions asked of these execs were, "What genre of script is easiest to write?" and, "What genre of script is the most difficult to write?" To the question of which genre of script is the easiest to write, 19 of the 20 execs gave the answer "Drama." To the question of which genre of script is the most difficult to write, 18 of the 20 said "Comedy." This begs the question: if it's apparently much easier to write drama than comedy, why does the Academy Award for best screenplay typically go to a dramatic script? This information should also let you know that you stand a better chance of distinguishing yourself as a filmmaker if you make a good comedy film rather than a good dramatic film. So write a drama if it's something you really must do, but if comedy or horror is an option for you, go that route instead.

A Final Note on Your Script

When you do begin to share your script with potential cast and crew members, you may get some people who tell you they don't want to be part of the film because they don't think your script is any good. Don't let this deter you.

This has happened to me. It actually happened to me twice with *Therapissed* alone, one of our comedy films. For two of the main roles in the film, I had very specific people in mind, but both of them, after reading the script, informed me that they didn't think the script was any good so they didn't want to be in the film. It did get me down for a little while (a few hours), but I quickly put their thoughts behind me, cast other people in the roles, and made a film that quickly landed a distribution deal.

Some people may not understand your script, or they may have a very different sense of humor than yours. Don't let this keep you from making your film. If you believe in your film and believe in your talents, make your film. Does belief in your talents and your script guarantee that you will make a good film? Certainly not. But it is a huge step in the right direction, and at the absolute minimum, for your film to have any chance at all of being well made and finding a release somewhere, you'd better believe without question that you have a script worthy of being turned into a film.

CHAPTER 2

Funding

Since you're making a small-budget film, you should be able to finance the film on your own, which not only keeps things much simpler from a producing vantage point (you don't have to hit up friends and family for money, you don't have to worry about SEC paperwork, etc.), but if you completely fund the film yourself, you will be the one who reaps the rewards from your film should it end up making money, which is much better than getting some money from some guy you barely know and seeing him be the one who profits from your film.

So how do you go about raising this money? You live frugally. While some of you may have an extra $1500 to $2000 lying about that you can simply tap into to make your film, many of you don't. And if you plan to make a couple of films in the next year, you might be looking at having to set aside $4000 to make your films, so here are some tips for making sure you have the money you need to make your films.

First, if you're not married, don't get married. If you are married, don't take on any extra lovers. Spouses and lovers cost money to keep happy, so keep them to an absolute minimum.

Second, don't have kids. If you do have kids, don't have any more. There aren't many things more expensive than children, so avoid having them at all costs.

Third, don't date, or if you must, keep your relationships on the casual side and don't get serious. Serious partners usually like to go out and do things, which costs money that you could be putting toward your next film.

When it comes to dating, I've read about a major Hollywood filmmaker who never dates a woman for more than two or three weeks before putting the relationship to an end. For filmmakers, this is smart for two reasons. One, while this filmmaker doesn't have to worry about money because of all the box office success he's had, you might have to worry about money, and not having a steady girlfriend or boyfriend will save you money. And two, serious girlfriends and boyfriends take up a lot of your time, as do spouses and children. When you need to pour yourself into a script and put together a cast and crew and set aside shoot days to get your film made, partners and children can get in the way. I know some seriously talented people who, because of family commitments, can't put the time and effort they would like to into their film endeavors. Don't let this happen to you.

Fourth, don't take on any large expenditures. This especially goes for mortgages and cars. Unless you have money falling out of your pockets on a daily basis, don't buy a house or a condo or any dwelling that requires you to get a mortgage. Why? Because mortgages mean you have to get a high-paying, full-time job to pay the mortgage, and high-paying, full-time jobs are public enemy number one when it comes to being a filmmaker. Those high-paying jobs typically always require at least 40 hours of work each week, and frequently much more than that, which leaves little to no time to write your script, put together your cast and crew, line up locations, and shoot your film. And keep in mind that when you take on a spouse and/or kids, you're much more likely to feel that pressure to buy a house, get a mortgage, and work at a good job, all of which spells death for your filmmaking endeavors. So when it comes to housing, find an inexpensive apartment where your monthly rent will be one-third to one-quarter of what a mortgage payment is, and you'll also save hundreds of dollars a month on utilities, taxes, insurance, and maintenance.

Cars are also an unnecessary burden to your filmmaking career. While not as onerous as a mortgage, buying a new car can saddle you with hefty car and insurance payments for years and quickly set you back in your efforts to raise the money you need to make your film. I have never paid more than $4000 for a car in my life, and this has given me a lot of economic flexibility and gone a long way toward allowing me to set aside the money I need to make films. And before you denounce the noble used car as a money pit of repairs that only lasts for a year or two, every inexpensive used car I've ever owned (and I've bought cars for as little as $1500) has lasted me at least three years, and only one of those cars has ever required much more than standard maintenance and repair. Drive these cars until they're shot, and then trade them in on another used car—it'll do wonders for your bank account.

A final way to easily save lots of money to make sure you can make your film is to stop going out for food and alcohol. These two items can add up to hundreds of extra dollars a month that you don't need to spend. Will your social life suffer? Of course. But you're a filmmaker, not a social butterfly. Go to the grocery store and stock up on rice, beans, and other items that can easily be turned into an inexpensive meal. It's not glamorous, but it very well could be that necessary step toward you making your next film. And don't go to bars. I've seen people quickly and easily drop $50 to $100 in a few hours in a bar between their drinks, drinks they buy for others, and tips. If you're a partier and like to hit the nightclubs and bars two or three times a week, just a few months of cutting nightclub and bar excursions out of your life might be all it takes for you to save up the money you need to make your film.

Another unnecessary expenditure many new filmmakers make that can really set them back in raising the $2000 they need to make their film is to get insurance coverage and legal advice for their films. If you're making films for $2000 or less, you don't have to worry about someone suing you for everything you have, because you probably don't have much. And if you're going to have some scenes in your film where someone could theoretically get hurt, simply have them sign a waiver saying that they acknowledge the fact that they will be doing something during the course of the filming of your movie that could lead to an injury, but that they will not hold you responsible for any injuries they might incur during the shoot. I did this with my film *To Die is Hard*. In the film there are four fight scenes, and I simply had each cast member who was involved in a fight scene sign a waiver saying they wouldn't hold me liable should they get hurt during the making of the film. The waiver was just a few sentences long, I wrote it myself (I didn't go to a lawyer and spend $500 to have him do it), and no one got hurt on set anyway since we took precautions to keep everyone safe. So don't spend more money on lawyers and insurance than you spend on the film itself. In fact, you probably shouldn't spend anything at all on lawyers and insurance when you make your film.

Finally, and this may be the most important part of the process when it comes to getting your film made, don't work too many hours each week. Yes, this is an extremely thin line you're walking between making sure you have the money

you need to make your film but also having the time you
need to make your film, but it's all but a necessity. Full-time
jobs make it much more difficult to get your film made, so if
you can find a job that lets you work only two to four days a
week, yet still brings in a fair amount of money and allows
flexibility in your schedule (did someone just say "waiter"?),
take that job. I'm fortunate in that I have a master's degree
that allows me to be a part-time college professor. Do I make
a ton of money? Hardly. Do I have benefits? Not one. But
I do only have to teach two days a week for 32 weeks out
of the year, and by living simply, that allows me to easily set
aside plenty of time and money to make my films.

At this point I'm sure many of you are thinking that
instead of making sacrifices, you'll simply go out and raise
the money to make your film from private investors or businesses (typically through product placement when it comes
to businesses); that you're not worried about sharing the
profits your film might make, you just want to make your
film; and that you want to have much more than $2000 at
your disposal to make your film. A very small percentage of
independent filmmakers will be able to convince individuals
and businesses to ante up thousands of dollars to help them
make their film. But for the most part, unless you have a big
name already signed on, those days of prolific fundraising
to make independent films are in the past.

I have heard tales from multiple cast and crew members who were active in the indie film world back in the mid-1990s and into the first couple of years of the 21st century about what it was like to raise money to make films back then. On the heels of the notoriety that independent films like *Clerks* and *The Blair Witch Project* garnered, there were people all over the country who were willing to throw thousands, sometimes tens of thousands, of dollars at indie filmmakers since the thought was floating around that investing in independent films was a great way to make a lot of money. When the advent of the Internet was factored into the equation (everyone was going to make a million dollars off the Internet, right?), it became a Golden Age for independent filmmakers to raise plenty of money to make their films, no matter how awful their scripts might be. But those days are long gone. With the way the economy is now, and with the plethora of independent filmmakers out there, it is nearly impossible to find investors for indie films. In fact, I've never even been able to talk a coffee shop or restaurant into donating free coffee or food to one of my shoots in exchange for a "thank you" in the film's credits, so don't count on private investors or businesses to foot the bill in the making of your film. It's up to you to make the necessary sacrifices to get your film made and to, hopefully, reap the financial rewards of your efforts.

One side note. Something to keep in mind for down the road when you do have bigger budgets to work with is to remember those cast and crew members who worked for you for almost nothing when you were starting out, and reward them with cast and crew positions that pay them well when you get to the point where you have hundreds of thousands or even millions of dollars to work with. These talented people made big sacrifices to work on your film or films when you had only a micro-budget to work with, so when you do have the opportunity to pay people well for working on your films, don't forget to include these people in your projects and pay them as much as you can for their work.

There are hundreds of ways to go about living a simpler life so you can save the money you need to make your film and find the time to write your script and make the film. It will take some sacrifice, and you will have to pass on some fun times with your friends. But keep this in mind: you can go out and party or eat at a restaurant any time you want for the rest of your life, but the time to make your film is now.

CHAPTER 3

Preproduction

So now you have your script in place and some money set aside to make your film. Now you have to get everything in place to shoot your film.

In making a small-budget film, you will more than likely handle all of your own producing. For me, this is my least favorite part of the filmmaking process as I would rather concern myself with the creative aspects of making a film, but producing is also a necessary step toward getting your film made.

There are various aspects to preparing for the shoot, and I will address them one at a time.

Your Cast

I find this aspect of the process to be a lot of fun, though it can be harrowing at times as well.

When I made my first short film, I posted a couple of notices on the Internet stating that I was making a short film, and that I needed to cast some people for the film. I was quickly inundated with dozens of responses, typically in the form of headshots and resumes. Actors and actresses like to work, even for nothing or next to nothing, so it shouldn't be a problem getting people to audition for you.

The audition process was fun. After sorting through all the headshots and resumes, I invited a few dozen people in to audition. While there were some people who auditioned who were certainly not ready to appear in a film, I also had many extremely talented people show up to try to land a spot in the cast, and I had to say no to quite a few of them. One thing I did notice, however, was that there were a lot more women out there wanting to act than men, especially when it comes to guys older than thirty, at least in the Denver area where I make my films. With this in mind, as you're writing your scripts, you may want to slightly limit the number of male roles, since it's usually easier to find women to be in your films.

One thing to keep in mind when casting your film is to not get caught up in emotions when handing out roles to people. This can happen primarily in two regards. First, you might want to give a role to a friend of yours, not because they're the best person for the role, but because they're your friend. While you might be able to get away with this (especially if it's a smaller role), more often than not the film is going to suffer because of such a move. If your friend really wants a role but they're not right for it, diplomatically explain to them why you're giving the role to someone else and hope your friend is understanding. In all likelihood your friend will get upset at the time, but eventually they'll realize you made the decision based upon what you thought was best for the film, and they will no longer take what you did as a personal assault. They'll get over it, and you'll be able to use him or her in a future project when they are the right person for a role.

The second thing you need to keep in mind when casting is not to give a role to an actor or actress simply because they're gorgeous or handsome. Yes, I have fallen prey to this, particularly with my first couple of projects. I would be holding auditions and a gorgeous woman would come in. She'd smile, maybe flirt the tiniest bit, my heart would melt, and before she had read even a single line, I was picturing her in the lead role of the film. Thankfully, on the few occasions this happened to me, not only were the gorgeous women who auditioned exceedingly talented, but another gorgeous woman typically auditioned just a short while later, and I most certainly couldn't cast two or three women all in the lead role. I was also thankful that I didn't get so swept away with any of these women that I offered them a role right on the spot, which could have eventually put me in a corner. Make sure you always let everyone on your slate audition before offering anyone a role. The best person for the role might be the first person to audition, but also might be the very last person to audition.

You also want to keep an eye out for those actors and actresses who are willing to do just about anything in a film to make it better (especially if you're making comedies). A great example I can give of this is with Lauren von Engeln, who played a leading role in *To Die is Hard* and is the featured female in our sketch comedy TV show *Driving With Our Eyes Shut*. As best as I can tell, Lauren is willing to take on any role, even if it means she might look like an idiot or do something that most people would consider embarrassing. If you can find a handful of talented and uninhibited actors or actresses like this, use them in your films whenever you get the chance.

Let me take a moment to address an issue that I get razzed about all the time. Many people are under the assumption that when you make films, all kinds of actresses are willing to sleep with you to land a role. Maybe this happens in Hollywood, where landing a role could mean a paycheck in the hundreds of thousands or millions of dollars, or where the role could mean getting a huge break that leads to making millions of dollars and being famous. But when you're offering $50 or $100 to be in a small-budget independent film, women (or guys for that matter) aren't interested is sleeping with you or pleasuring you in any way to get a role. So if you're thinking that making films will be a great way to hook up with some gorgeous babes, don't count on it.

Another casting aspect to be open to is casting someone in a role that you might not have originally thought would work. For example, when I wrote the script for *The Worst Movie EVER!* I had a very specific actress in mind to play the role of Angela, the soul taker's assistant. She was a woman well into her twenties, and she had worked on previous projects with me and done a great job. However, when I set the shooting schedule, she informed me she couldn't make the shoot that weekend (we shot the film in one weekend), so I was left to find someone else to fill the role. A week later, I still didn't have the role filled, and I was beginning to worry a little bit about who would play the role. Then by chance I crossed paths with a young actress named Christine Mascolo whose friend, Haidyn Harvey, had been one of the stars of one of our previous films, *To Die is Hard*. Christine informed me that she would like to be in one of my films one day. I began to think that maybe it would work quite well if Laduelia, the soul taker (played by Eileen Barker), had a young apprentice as her assistant, so I cast Christine, who was 13 years old, in that role. It worked out great as Christine brought a whole new dimension to the role that I hadn't envisioned and that really added to the film.

I also found myself on the receiving end of some other casting good fortune when it came to *To Die is Hard*. I thought I had the cast in place when the actor I had cast as the lead terrorist, Anton, had to pull out of the film just a couple weeks before we began filming. I was convinced that this actor was perfect for the role, and I was devastated he wouldn't be in the film. As it turned out, I switched actor Baird Lefter from playing the role of tough-guy terrorist Stewart to that of cerebral lead terrorist Anton, and moved actor Will Beckingham from being the largely quiet terrorist Turk into the role of tough-guy Stewart. It could not have worked out more perfectly as both Baird and Will delivered fantastic performances and completely nailed their characters, while Stuart Goldstein stepped in to play Turk and did an outstanding job.

Always keep your mind open when it comes to filling your cast. You may find that someone auditions for you who would be perfect for a particular role, only they're the wrong sex. If that's the case, go back to your script, do a quick rewrite where you change the sex of that character, and cast that actor or actress in the role. This happened with the character of Andrea in *To Die is Hard*, which in the first draft of the film was a male named Andre until I realized that actress Ashley Henkle would be perfect in the role, so Andre became Andrea. If an actor who you thought was indispensable to the film has to bow out for some reason, don't despair, as this may open up the door for someone else who ends up being even better in the role than the actor you originally cast for it.

Also keep a close eye on those actors and actresses who have small roles in your films. You might find that someone who's playing a character who only has a scene or two does a fantastic job with their role and that they might be great in a much more substantial role in a future film of yours. And if this cast member is also punctual and has all of their lines down (basically meaning that they conduct themselves as a professional), then you have a real winner on your hands who you need to keep using in your future filmmaking endeavors.

Two great examples of this are Ashley Henkle and Stephanie VanGels, who played Andrea and Sandy, respectively, in *To Die is Hard*. They had both been in one of the first short films I made, and Ashley had also appeared in a small role in my feature film *Therapissed*. They're both very talented, they're both professional, and they're both easy to work since they have great personalities. Why wouldn't I want to work with them again?

The same can be said for other actors and actresses I've worked with. Will Beckingham, Eileen Barker, Baird Lefter, Giovanna Leah, Hip Hop Joe Filippone, Jon Jorgensen, Elena Chin, and many others initially only had very small roles in my early productions but ended up playing bigger roles in later films. So from a filmmaker's perspective, always be paying attention to everyone in your cast and how they comport themselves. And if you're an actor who's reading this book, you'd better know that your director is taking notice of whether or not you're showing up on time, whether

or not you know your lines, and whether or not the other
people involved in the making of the film are enjoying having you on set.

Keep in mind as well that someone who may have auditioned for you long ago but not been cast might be right
for a role in the next film you're about to make. The best
example of this for me is with the actress Laurie Clemens.
She auditioned for *Bad Movies, Good Showers, and Civil Engineers* but didn't seem quite right for either of the roles she
was up for. More than a year and a half later I thought she
would be great in the role of Eileen in *Therapissed*. I offered
her the role, she accepted, and she turned in a fantastic performance. So don't forget about those actors and actresses
you maybe haven't crossed paths with in a while as one of
them might be perfect for the next film you shoot.

Also keep in mind that you don't necessarily have to always even use experienced actors in your film, that using
your non-acting friends can be an inexpensive way to round
out your cast. The best example I can give of this is my best
buddy Jeff McBride. Jeff and I go back over 20 years to
when we played baseball together. Jeff is a funny guy. Had
he ever acted before when I asked him to be in one of my
projects? No, but he gladly accepted my invitation to act
in a smaller role in our sketch comedy TV show *Driving
With Our Eyes Shut*, and he did a great job, especially in the
sketch where John McEnroe and Jesus play doubles tennis

together. Since Jeff did such a good job on the TV show, I have since cast him in both *To Die is Hard* and *The Worst Movie EVER!* and he's done a great job in those projects as well. I've also brought in friends like Christopher Irvin, Jeff Johnson, and Carla Cannalte to be in my films. Christopher, Jeff, and Carla were all inexperienced actors when I cast them in *The Worst Movie EVER!* but all of them threw themselves into their characters and delivered fantastic performances.

If you do end up casting some inexperienced actors in your film, I have found that one little simple bit of advice seems to work well with them. Your inexperienced cast members will typically be very nervous because they're worried about their performance, they're worried about messing up a take by forgetting their lines, and they're worried about messing up the movie by giving a poor performance. All I tell them, if they seem a bit extra nervous, is that acting is no more than pretending to be someone else for a little while. We've all pretended to be someone else at some point in our lives, even if we have to hearken back to when we were children and playing cops and robbers or cowboys and Native Americans. You're playing Dr. Dirk Ramrod in this film? Then simply pretend you're a scientist for a couple of hours. You're playing a slightly scared professor who's trapped in a building that terrorists have taken over? Then simply pretend for a couple hours that you're a slightly scared professor who's trapped in a building. Telling your rookies that acting is no more than pretending to be someone else frequently helps put their minds at ease and takes away at least some of their worries.

This brings us to the issue of whether you should consider casting yourself in your film. The answer—yes!

When I was casting my first film, the short film *Bad Movies, Good Showers, and Civil Engineers*, I didn't have as many men audition as I'd hoped. While I did have quite a few younger guys audition for the three roles of college-aged guys, when it came to finding someone for the small role of the Bored Man, I had one person audition, and he just wasn't right for the role. As the shoot date drew near, I came to the decision that I would have to play the role. While I was nervous about this since I had never acted before, I figured I could handle the three lines that the Bored Man had.

When the shoot day arrived and it came time to shoot my scenes, I found that it was no big deal to act in my scenes. I told myself that for the next little while I would simply pretend I was the Bored Man. My scenes turned out fine. Of course, it didn't hurt that I had the very professional and incredibly talented Eileen Barker acting in the scenes with me.

After that I began casting myself in more substantial supporting roles. Was this because I loved acting? No. I liked acting, and I was having fun doing it. And I'm always up for the challenge of pulling off a good performance. But as a small-budget independent filmmaker, there are two main benefits to casting yourself in your film—you save money by having one less person to pay, and you eliminate one more variable in the process: worrying about an actor showing up and knowing their lines, which, believe you me, has happened to me multiple times over the years.

What I found as well with casting myself is that I began to enjoy the acting process more and more, to the point where I went from playing smaller roles in *Evil Intent* and *Therapissed* to playing the lead role in both *To Die is Hard* and *The Worst Movie EVER!* If you know you'll be playing a particular role in your film, while writing your script you can tailor your character's lines to what you're comfortable with, whether that means keeping your lines short and simple and spreading them out throughout the film, or giving yourself fewer scenes but giving yourself more lines over the course of those scenes.

And one other note. If you have dreams of landing a big Hollywood name in your film, don't hold your breath. With a budget of $2000 or less, you're not getting anyone from Hollywood to be in your film, no matter how great the script is. But if you have some success with this film and are able to get a budget for your next film that's in the hundreds of thousands or millions of dollars, you might be able to land that star you've long wanted to work with. And don't feel bad that you're only paying your cast members a pittance

to be in your film—when you gain enough notoriety to get
a substantial budget to make a film, use these same cast
members again, and pay them a good wage for their work
then to make up for the work they're doing for you now.

Your Crew

Here is where you can really save a lot of money over what
other filmmakers will say you have to spend to make your
film. There are two people in the crew who are absolutely
integral to making a good film: the director of photography
(DP) and the editor. While one can debate which is more
important, I give a slight nod to the editor as being more
vital to making sure the film turns out as you want it to.

In my early films I frequently had two, and often three,
camera people shooting on set at the same time. This is
convenient in that you can get a lot of footage from one
take, but it's not absolutely necessary. In my last few films
I've simply gone with one cameraperson, who also serves
as DP. With a DP serving in this capacity, they can typically
move quickly to get the over-the-shoulder and close-up
shots they and you want, which really doesn't slow down
the shoot at all. Compare this to having two or three cameras all rolling at the same time: when you have three
cameras going, you usually end up spending extra time
setting up each shot on each camera to make sure you can't
see the other cameras or their tripod legs in frame, which

sometimes can add a couple extra minutes to setting up almost every shot.

It is important to have a DP on board who you can trust. While in Hollywood they might be able to get away with shooting two pages of script in a day, you don't have that luxury. You can't have your DP play back shots for you after each take or your film will never get done. You have to trust that the DP is getting the necessary footage. Might this lead to you getting burned on occasion? Certainly. But if you take the time to interview multiple DPs before settling on one, and if you take the time to watch their demo reels, you should be safe in this regard. You also want your DP to be someone you can trust to know the ins and outs of aspect ratios and frame rates and all that other stuff that I know little to nothing about. If you want to learn all about how cameras work, that's fine, but I'd rather focus on the script and the shoot and let my DP and editor worry about those things.

When it comes to the editor, I always pay the editor more than anyone else who works on the film. Why? Because the editor will end up putting in many more hours on the film than anyone else, and they should be compensated as such. As a general rule, I would say I end up giving to the editor about one-third of the budget for a film. Even with that, in most cases that will probably work out to a matter of $5 an hour or less for all the work they end up doing.

When it comes to a sound person for your film, you can use just about anyone for this role. If you have a microphone with a boom (we often just duct tape the mic to a golf club), all they have to do is point the microphone in the direction of the person or people speaking in the scene. With about thirty seconds of training, nearly anyone can handle this job. In fact, to save even more money, feel free to handle the boom yourself. While some directors might think this is degrading, it's not, and it's a job that must be done. And by doing it yourself, that's one less crew member to pay and one less person you have to worry about showing up on time.

When it comes to lighting, keep it simple. If you're shooting outside during the day, you don't need anyone to handle lighting. If you're shooting inside during the day, natural lighting will usually be adequate. If you're shooting inside during the night, the house lights on hand are often enough, and if they're not, one or two well-placed lamps will usually be enough to give you the light you need to shoot the scene. (I typically have two directional lamps on hand—one with a 200-watt bulb and one with a 75- or 100-watt bulb.) If you're shooting outside at night, you might need to bring a lighting expert on board, but outside night shots are a pain in the butt, so I rarely include them in my scripts.

By not using a lighting technician you can save some money on your shoot, and most DPs know how to light a scene as well. On top of that, if there is one thing that can really slow down your shoot, it's the lighting. With all the equipment and wires and extension cords, by the time the scene is blocked to appease the lighting tech and everything is in place and all the cords are taped down so no one trips over them, your film will be falling way behind schedule. And when you factor in that if you use a lighting tech you will be going through this process over and over all day long, all that wasted time is just not worth it.

But what about shadows? You can't have shadows on the set, right? And you need an experienced lighting technician to make sure you don't have shadows on your set, correct? Wrong. Keep in mind that the myth that you can't have any shadows on set is just that, a myth. Look around you, and you'll see there are shadows everywhere all the time. Shadows are part of life, so they can certainly be part of your film as long as they don't fall across an actor's face.

You also don't need anyone in your crew whose job it is to handle wardrobe or makeup. By keeping your scripts simple with regular people doing normal things (for the most part), you don't need anyone to handle wardrobe. Simply tell each cast member what you want them to wear, and then have them bring some outfits with them to the rehearsal that fit what you're looking for. In a matter of moments you can let them know which outfits work for the film and which ones don't. And by handling wardrobe in this manner, you don't have to waste money paying someone to do something that is so easily handled by you and your cast members.

With makeup, hiring someone to handle this is a waste of time and money. All the women in your cast will know how to do their own makeup, and pretty much all guys look fine without makeup. And by eliminating a makeup person, you not only save money on not having to pay a person to do this unnecessary job, you also save money by having one less person to feed, and you save time by having one less person on set who will be demanding your time and attention during the shoot.

It is sometimes nice to have a production assistant around to help out on set. While not mandatory, they can come in handy when it comes to helping move equipment or furniture around, for filling in for the boom guy when he shows up late or has to leave early, or for any of numerous other tasks that need to be taken care of on set. But limit yourself to just one PA as this will not only save you money, but the fewer people you have on set, the faster your shoot will move along. This means you don't need to bring on a key grip, a second assistant director, a line producer, or any of the other dozens of roles that most filmmakers waste their time and money to bring on board. When it comes to making small-budget films, these crew members are completely unnecessary.

Finally, when it comes to your crew (and cast) members, remember three things. One, as the filmmaker, if you surround yourself with talented people, it makes you look good. Two, only have people in your crew and cast who are happy, friendly people who are easy to work with. I don't care how talented someone might be, if they're angry, sullen, or like to yell a lot, they will not be any fun to work with and will bring down the entire shoot. It's my philosophy that if someone is a jerk even once, I don't bring them back to work on my films again. And three, never ever yell at someone on the crew or in the cast. Everyone on set wants the film to turn out well, and everyone wants to do a good job, so even if someone messes up, or keeps messing up, keep smiling and encouraging everyone, and the shoot will go much better than if you begin to yell at people. Trust me on this.

Permits

I have one general rule when it comes to getting permits and permission to shoot somewhere—I don't get them!

For two of my short films I did get permission to use rooms in campus buildings where I was a professor. It cost me nothing as I merely had to talk with the building supervisor, tell him when I wanted to shoot, and he merely made sure the door to the room was unlocked for me. Other than that, I've never secured permission to use a building, nor have I ever paid a fee to use a building or location. Here are some reasons why.

To start with, tracking down the person you need to speak with to get permission, and working out the details of when you can shoot, can be a real time consumer. It's not too bad if you're a professor and wanting to use a campus building, but if you're working with an outside organization or business, it can be a real hassle. And if you're dealing with a government agency of any sort, even if it's your local parks department, it's even more of a pain in the butt. I have a personal story on that.

A few years ago when we got around to shooting our sketch comedy TV show *Driving With Our Eyes Shut*, we had a sketch where, in a couple scenes of a sketch, we needed a youth baseball team to appear where one child had a couple lines. In talking with some people, one of my regular cast members, Eileen Barker, mentioned that her son played on a t-ball baseball team, and that the players and parents were in agreement that they would like to be in the sketch. I was thrilled with this news.

Eileen lives about twenty minutes away from me, and she suggested we shoot the scenes at the baseball field right by her that the team played on. That was fine with me, so I asked her when we could get everyone together. She said to let her check with the parks department first to see when we could get on the field. I suggested that if it was going to be a hassle to shoot on that field, we could shoot at a little base-ball field in a public park half a mile from my apartment.

Over the course of the next four weeks, Eileen was sent from one person to another about securing the use of the field. On top of that, the parks department wanted a substantial amount of paperwork filled out, we had to prove we had insurance (I've never had one bit of insurance for any project I've worked on), and we would have to pay a field rental fee ranging into the hundreds of dollars. Eileen finally had enough with the parks department. We brought the children over to the field by my apartment, we shot the scenes for free, without permission, and we got all the footage we needed.

When it came to our feature film *To Die is Hard*, I didn't have permission to shoot on the college campus where 90% of the film took place. I didn't even try to get permission, but whenever somebody asked me whether I had obtained permission or not, I simply said "Yes." This even worked with the guy from campus security who asked me what was going on the one morning we were shooting out in front of a campus building.

Now keep in mind that I wasn't being a complete renegade in either of these instances. When shooting the children on the baseball field, we went to the field at 10 in the morning on a weekday when no one was there, so we weren't interrupting any events or games. And when shooting on the college campus, we shot on two weekends during the summer when the campus was virtually empty, so, again, we were not disrupting any events or lives.

My favorite incident of not obtaining permission, however, has to do with a church and our short film *Guernica Still Burning*. *Guernica Still Burning* (which is based on a book I've had published) is about a young man who is questioning all that his parents have taught him, including the religious teachings they instilled in him. There are a couple of short scenes in the film where he's in a church by himself. There is no dialogue in these scenes, just voice-over.

I approached a conveniently located church to inquire about going into their sanctuary for 15 minutes or so one day to get these shots. I was informed that not only would the church require script approval (which I'm sure they wouldn't have given me), but they also wanted $285 for a one-hour rental of the sanctuary (billing was in one-hour increments). I wasn't going to do that.

On the second and final day of the shoot, I decided we should go by this church (which left its doors unlocked during the day so people could enter to pray) and see if we could shoot the scenes. So while I stood watch outside, Alan Dague-Greene, the DP on the film, ran into the sanctuary with his camera while Jason W. Griffith, the lead actor in the film, went in with him. In 15 minutes' time they had all the shots they needed. We quickly hopped back into our cars and went on our way, guerrilla film-making at its finest.

It's amazing how people will defer to a few guys when one of them has a camera. And even if you do get questioned about whether you have permission or not, a confident "Yes, we do" always seems to do the trick. And what if you do get busted? Should that happen, you'll probably just be asked to leave, which could be a hassle but which can be worked around. But if you plan to shoot in a privately owned business, you most certainly better make sure you have permission to film there.

Keep in mind, however, that if you plan to use a busy city street for your shoot, that's a whole other basket of kittens. If there's any chance at all that a police officer might question you, you might want to have some permits in order. I avoid this potential problem by simply writing scripts that don't contain any scenes on busy public streets.

Another example of where you will want to get a permit is if you plan to have actual guns on set. Guns in public without the proper paperwork can lead to huge problems, including jail time. But there's an easy way around this—use squirt guns! In *To Die is Hard* we used all plastic guns that I bought for a few dollars and spray painted black. The one exception was the gun Will Beckingham used in the film, which was a BB gun. However, I've heard of guys who want to make a film, and for the sake of authenticity, they want to have real guns on set. If this is an absolute must with you, just realize you will get bogged down with mounds of paperwork, you will have to spend months getting one person or department after another to give you approval for your shoot, and you will be dishing out copious amounts of money for permits and insurance, none of which are conducive to small-budget, fast-moving filmmaking.

What it comes down to is that you need to limit the number of locations in your film, and whenever possible shoot in the houses, apartments, and workplaces that you and your cast and crew members have ready access to. It keeps your costs down and your headaches to a minimum, and it allows you to avoid the hassles that come with dealing with municipalities and government offices.

Film or Digital?

Digital! This is not even a question, as there is no way you will be able to purchase and develop actual film for any amount that will keep you under your $2000 budget. In fact, if you are wed to the fact that you must use actual film for your movie, you're probably looking at a minimum of $10,000 or more just for that alone. Footage from digital cameras looks fantastic. And for $40 or $50, you can certainly purchase enough media to shoot your entire film, and you don't have to pay to have it developed.

Another growing option is to use a camera that records the footage onto a memory card. These are quite convenient, with the only exception being that the shoot has to come to a halt once or twice a day for about half an hour so the footage can be downloaded into a computer (this is a good time to take a food break). However, if you have access to multiple cards, this isn't a problem, as you can simply continue to shoot on the second card while the footage on the first card is being downloaded.

Storyboarding

For those who aren't aware, storyboarding is going through your script, planning out (with the assistance of your director of photography) each shot you want to get in your film—from close-ups to zoom-ins to over-the-shoulder shots to master shots to inserts to every other shot you want to get—and then having an artist make drawings of each of these hundreds of shots so that when you get on set, you know exactly where every cast member needs to be for every shot in the film and where your camera person needs to be to get every one of those shots.

I have read on multiple occasions that storyboarding is a must for a film, that it really speeds up the process once you get on set as there is no debate or discussion over blocking a scene or where the camera will be set up since all you have to do is consult the storyboards. That being said, I have never storyboarded one of my films.

First off, storyboarding each scene can take weeks to months to do if you have your artist draw up detailed storyboards. Second, if you're going to bring an artist on board who will have to spend weeks or months of their time drawing up the storyboards, you better be prepared to pay this person a fair amount of money, which could certainly put you over your intended budget.

Would storyboarding be effective in speeding up your shoot if you do it? Probably. And if you have millions of dollars at your disposal for making your film, and months and months of preproduction time to get it done, then go ahead and do it. But when you're working quickly and with a small budget, there's no need to storyboard. Here's why.

You will certainly have ideas for how you want each scene to be shot, and your director of photography will have some ideas as well. When you're on set and preparing to shoot a scene, and as your cast members go over their lines one last time and make any wardrobe changes they need to make, you can tell your DP how you want the scene shot.

Your DP will sometimes suggest ways he wants the scene to be shot. You can take 10 to 30 seconds to reach a final decision, and then set up for the shot. And since you're using only one or two cameras and one or two lights, setting up to shoot the scene will take mere moments.

You can also shoot on the fly like this when you realize your film isn't going to win an Academy Award for best cinematography. When making a small-budget film, simply get the shots that will allow you to tell your story. You don't need cool angles and bizarre lighting set-ups and a thousand inserts and cutaways, you need to capture the dialogue and capture what your characters are doing. This will typically consist of a master shot and a few close-ups and/or over-the-shoulder shots—don't make it harder than it has to be. And don't waste your time and money on storyboarding.

Props

On most every shoot you will have to bring at least a few props, possibly many more. These props are usually simple things like a bandana or a kitchen utensil or something small like that, but they're often integral to the shoot. For example, in *To Die is Hard*, I spent three dollars to purchase three plastic guns, and then spent another 88 cents to buy some cheap black spray paint to paint them with. Cheap props, yes, but also props that were absolutely necessary in the making of the film. Had I forgotten them, the shoot would have been extremely compromised. We would have either had to come to a stop for a while as I sent someone out to hurriedly buy and spray paint some plastic guns, or we would have had to find some kind of (probably) lame way to improvise guns on set.

When it comes to your props, you can frequently get many of them at second-hand stores or dollar stores, or you might even have some of them lying about in your house. Sometimes you can send out emails to cast and crew members and see if someone might have a particular item you need that might either be hard to find or rather expensive. Whatever you do, don't break the bank in buying a bunch of expensive props. I don't think I've ever spent more than $50 for the props for any film, and more often than not, I've been more in the $20 range for the props I purchased for a film.

Another option for more expensive props is to buy them new a week or so before they're needed, save the receipt and leave the price tag on them, and then return them the day after you're done using them. When we shot the sketch comedy show *Driving With Our Eyes Shut*, we ended up using a whole bunch of props, and I used this method for a number of the props in the show. In this manner I managed to save over $100 for the shoot. Certainly, this wasn't the proudest thing I've ever done in my life, but a small-budget filmmaker has to do what he has to do, and this bit of prop wrangling definitely helped make it possible for the show to be shot.

I try to make sure I have all the props in place at least a week or two prior to the commencing of filming. This way I don't have to stress out over them and spend time running around town trying to find the items I need in the days leading up to the shoot when I'll have plenty enough to concern myself with. Typically, as I assemble the props for the film, I'll simply put them in a single box or bag, and then check them off the list I made for all the props I need to get (I always check and recheck the script to make sure I don't miss out on any necessary props to include on my prop list). Once I have every item checked off the list (and I might slowly accumulate these things over the course of a couple of weeks), all I have left to do is make sure I take my box or bag of props with me to the shoot each day. Whatever you do, do not forget your prop box, or you'll have a major headache on your hands.

Your Shooting Schedule

I have always limited my shooting schedule to no more than two weekends' worth of filming, for multiple reasons. First, it's hard to ask people to commit to a long shoot when you're paying them very little money. Second, shooting on weekdays often means that people have to take off work to make it to the shoot. It's bad enough that you're only paying these people $50 or so to work on your film, and now you want them to miss work as well and eat into their paychecks? Don't do this.

It's also exciting to the cast and crew to shoot quickly, as they don't have to worry about the film getting bogged down for months, or even a year or more, just in trying to get the script shot. Your cast and crew are working hard for you, so you owe it to them to get the project finished in a timely manner.

Also keep in mind when making out your shoot schedule for each day that you should always make it for much longer than you think it will actually go. For example, if I think it'll take eight hours to get everything shot that we need to on a particular day, I'll schedule a 12-hour shoot day. This keeps spirits high for the day—when cast and crew see that you're ahead of schedule, they get excited that things are going so well. And if you do fall behind the pace you think you should be keeping, no one else realizes it, so no one gets upset. However, if you schedule an eight-hour day, and it gets to the point where you've been on set for 10 or 11 hours, people get cranky.

You'll also want to stagger your call times for cast members, and get them finished up and on their way as soon as possible. (This doesn't typically apply to crew members as they need to be on set all day for every scene—all the more reason to make sure you have happy, smiling, easy-to-work-with crew members.) If you can get someone in early and all their scenes shot in a couple hours, do that and get them off the set. If another cast member doesn't need to come in until noon, don't bring them in until then. The shoot can always move faster when there are fewer people around, and besides, you don't want to make a cast member wait around all day just to shoot a scene here or there if you can at all avoid it. This leads to bored and/or unhappy cast members, which isn't very conducive to having a good shoot.

Inevitably, however, there are always one or two cast members in each film who get hosed, no matter how you might try to accommodate each cast member to keep them from having to hang out on set for hours and hours between scenes. In the case of *The Worst Movie EVER!* that cast member was Kasha Fauscett. On both days of the shoot (we shot the film in one weekend), Kasha had to come in early and stay nearly to the end of the day as her character was in and out of the film in multiple locations and with multiple other cast members. But Kasha was a real professional about it, keeping an upbeat, happy attitude through the entire weekend. I, and everyone who was part of the crew and cast, really appreciated her being so wonderful about it. And once again, this is another reason why you should make sure you have happy, genial people in your film. If I had cast someone else in that role who wasn't happy and easygoing, it could have made for a lot of contentiousness on the set.

When it comes to setting up your shooting schedule, try to lump cast members together first, and then try to accommodate locations second. Obviously, if you're shooting in two locations 20 miles apart over the course of one weekend, you'll shoot all the scenes of one location on one day, then all the other location scenes the next day. However, if you're shooting multiple locations in the same house on a particular day, accommodate the cast first. For example, don't be afraid to jump around from room to room in the house to get one or two cast members' scenes all finished up so you can get them on their way. If you're using a skeleton crew of you, a DP, and a boom operator with just a couple of extra lights, jumping around from room to room is very easy to do. By getting those cast members finished up early, you'll keep them happy, and it'll be easy to move back to a room you already shot in to shoot other scenes with other cast members.

Another thing I've learned over the years is that teen cast members bring a lot of energy to the set. I've only worked with a few of them, but they're always excited to be making a film. This knowledge can come in handy when setting up your schedule in the regard that if you bring the teens onto the set later in the day, it can give a real boost to the set and reenergize the crew. A mistake I made on the set of *The Worst Movie EVER!* was to have the three teens in the film—Haidyn Harvey, Bryce Foster, and Christine Mascolo—come in at the very start of the day (or at least early in the day) on both days of the shoot. Four hours later, when they were all finished and out the door, for a short while it felt like the life had been sucked off the set as much of the giggling, laughter, and energy that had been around all morning suddenly disappeared. Both times we quickly recovered and had a great time shooting over the next few hours, but if I had it to do over again, I would have brought Haidyn, Bryce, and Christine in later so that the crew could have fed off of their energy as the day moved on.

The Rehearsal

I typically hold my rehearsals in my apartment, somewhere between two days to two weeks prior to the beginning of shooting the film. I try to accomplish a number of things with the rehearsal.

To start with, as cast members arrive for the rehearsal, I give them whatever money I promised them to be in the shoot (most of the time I pay everyone in the cast—from leading man down to those people who are in only one or two scenes—the exact same amount of money), and I have each cast member sign a release form to be in the film. What is the release form? It's a very simple form saying that I can use their image in any manner I deem appropriate for the making of the film and for promotional reasons. The form I use I simply printed off the Internet (there are dozens of them to choose from), and most cast members simply sign the form without reading it. I always have them sign one copy for me, and I have them keep one copy for themselves. Getting all of the paperwork and payments out of the way at this point allows you the freedom to not have to worry about them during the shoot.

Next on the agenda is to pass out call sheets. By the time of the rehearsal I have made out a detailed list of what scenes will be shot in which locations in which order on what days and which cast members I need on set at what times. Cast members like to be able to be well prepared once filming begins, and making sure everyone knows exactly what is going on at all times allows them to be more relaxed and do a better job. In addition, a detailed schedule shows your cast and crew that you are well prepared and in control (believe me, your cast and crew wants a director who is in control and guiding the project), which raises their spirits that all will go well with the shoot. A happy cast and crew makes for a great shoot.

The third thing I do is to check on each actor and actress's wardrobe. I ask my cast members to wear an outfit to the rehearsal that they think will work for their character, and I ask them to bring a few other outfits as well that I can look over. This is a very simple and efficient way for taking care of all wardrobe issues before filming even begins.

Once all of these matters have been taken care of and everyone who wants something to eat or drink has been able to get a little something (I always have a few simple snacks and beverages available for the rehearsal), we begin our read-through. For a feature film, the read-through typically takes around an hour and a half or so.

It is during the rehearsal that I typically do most of my directing. Sometimes I do the directing right during the rehearsal, letting cast members know if I want a little different voice inflection for their character or in a particular scene, taking a moment to explain how I want a scene to play out, etc. With cast members who might be a little sensitive, or if it's something that might be at all embarrassing to the cast member, I'll either take them off to the side later and tell them what I'm looking for, or I'll send them an email the next day with my thoughts. As the writer/director/producer of the film, you need to always make sure you treat your cast and crew members with courteousness and respect. Should you embarrass a cast member in any way, especially in front of other people involved in the film, you will have an unhappy cast member on your hands who you will probably not get a great performance out of.

One thing you will frequently get from your cast members are suggestions for things they want to do with their character, or for things they want to add to the script. Be open to these suggestions. You will have some very talented people working on your film, and they sometimes proffer forth some great suggestions that improve your film. But in this regard you also need to be judicious. It's been my experience that 80% or more of the comments and suggestions cast and crew members make won't do anything to help the film, and in some cases may detract from what you're trying to accomplish. Remember—this is your film, and it will have your name on it, so make it the way you want to. If a cast member suggests something that you don't want to incorporate into the film, politely let them know that you don't think their suggestion will work for the way you have the scene or film envisioned. I've found that cast and crew members are usually not the least bit offended by you refusing one of their suggestions as long as you do it politely and tactfully.

I frequently bring my crew members in for the rehearsal as well. They will typically go off to the side and go over the things they need to go over (with the director of photography leading the meeting) to be ready for the shoot. When they're finished, the DP frequently then joins us for the rest of the read-through so he can get some ideas for some shots he wants to get once we get to filming.

When it comes to crew members, they will also sometimes makes suggestions for things they think might be nice to add to the film, whether their suggestion is in the form of a shot they would like to see, a particular way to block out a scene, or whatever. Just like with cast members, be open to their suggestions while also keeping in mind that it is your film and your vision.

At the conclusion of the rehearsal, remind everyone of when and where they need to be once filming begins, and be prepared to answer a whole bunch of questions, whether the questions come in front of everyone while the cast is still present, or whether the questions come one-on-one from cast or crew members as the group begins to disperse. On most occasions, after answering all the questions, the last two people left are me and the DP, and we typically chat for a few more minutes to answer questions either of us might have.

The rehearsal should be a lot of fun. It's a chance to play with the script a little bit, to do a lot of laughing (especially if the film you're about to shoot is a comedy), and for cast and crew members who haven't worked together in a while to catch up on things. Let this be a fun evening for everyone, and you'll set the tone for a great shoot.

Summary

Your preproduction work is a lot of tediousness, but it's a must for your film to get made. Pay close attention to the details so that nothing (or at least as little as possible) surprises you once you finally get around to making your film.

CHAPTER 4

The Shoot

When making your small-budget film, you need to get all 90 or so pages of your script shot in a matter of days, not weeks or months. While we've all heard tales of big-budget films shooting at a snail's pace of two or three pages of script per day, or even less, you don't have that luxury. (My personal favorite is the cast member from *The Last Picture Show* who told the tale of the seven hours they took one day on set to shoot what turned out to be 10 seconds' worth of the film.) I don't know the exact page amount that would constitute the most pages we've ever shot in a single day, but it would be somewhere around 40 to 45 pages.

There are many variables that come into play that allow a filmmaker to shoot this quickly. Let's address them one at a time.

Arrive Early

As the director and producer, you better be the first one on set, and you better make sure you have access to the places you need to shoot for the day. Should you plan to shoot in

a friend's house and arrive to find the house is locked and
no one is home, you better be there early enough to make
sure you get that house unlocked before anyone else arrives. And if you're shooting in a public building, you better make sure you're there early enough to make sure you
can get in as well.

You also need to make sure your director of photography and sound person arrive early as well, so they can get
set up and be ready to go when the cast begins to arrive.
While they're setting up their equipment and getting your
one or two extra lights in place, you can set up the craft
services, otherwise known as the food. It's with the food
that you set out for the shoot where many filmmakers waste
a lot of money.

Yes, it would be nice to have food catered in for your
shoot, and many filmmakers spend hundreds and hundreds, even thousands, of dollars doing this. However, you
can feed a cast and crew of fifteen people on $20 for an en-
tire weekend. How? Go to a dollar store or discount grocery
store and buy some bags of chips and pretzels, some granola
bars, some crackers, some mini candy bars, some bananas,
and a bottle or two of juice, and you're set. How can you get
by on this? First off, most cast members will only be on set
for three to six hours (if you've done a good job of schedul-
ing), so they won't need a major meal during this time, just
something to nibble on. And the two or three crew members

who are on set all day long won't have time for a sit-down meal, but it is easy for them to grab a snack every hour or so and keep working. This is how you can keep your costs to an absolute minimum when it comes to food.

One perk you can try to make available that won't ruin your budget is to have a coffeemaker on hand. While many cast and crew members will stop at a coffee shop on their way to the shoot, if you have access to a coffeemaker and some coffee, bring that along. A fresh cup of coffee will go a long way toward keeping some of your cast and crew members exceedingly happy.

While Shooting

Since you are taking days and not weeks to shoot your film, you need to have everyone available to you that you need, and you need to move quickly. Make sure you have the phone numbers of all cast and crew members with you in case someone should be late. Don't wait too long to put a call in to a tardy cast or crew member. If someone is 15 or 30 minutes late, give them a quick call to make sure they're on their way—you will occasionally give a person a call to check on them and find they are still in bed. At least by calling them at this point, they should be able to get to the shoot no more than an hour and a half late, and while you wait for them to arrive, you can shoot other scenes where you do have everyone present that you need to shoot the scenes.

Just before you shoot your first scene of each day, make sure everyone on set has turned their phones off, and make sure you turn off any noisy appliances that might be close by, most specifically refrigerators, which can kick on in the middle of a scene and mess up your audio. Make sure, however, that at the end of the day you turn the refrigerator back on so you don't end up with a refrigerator and freezer filled with quickly spoiling food.

You also need to establish right off the bat that when a scene is ready to be shot, all conversations must come to an immediate end. What you will find is that many people on your cast and crew know each other in one way or another, so they'll want to chat about the films they've done together, what films they've worked on recently, if they know what a mutual friend has been up to lately, what films they're scheduled to work on in the coming months, etc. This is totally fine; however, these conversations need to cease immediately when you're ready to shoot—you can't be polite and let them go on for another minute or two before you break in and tell them the scene needs to be shot. Why can't you extend to your cast and crew this little nicety? Because if you're shooting 50 or 60 scenes in a day (which I've frequently done), and you waste a minute or two before each scene letting people chat, you're looking at adding an extra hour or two to your shoot each day, which, in a worst-case scenario, could mean not getting everything shot for the day and having to come back for an extra day of shooting, which no one wants. Or, in a best-case scenario, you've just turned your 10-hour shoot day into an 11- or 12-hour shoot day, and believe me, no one (including you) will be happy with making your day longer than it has to be.

This doesn't mean you have to be rude to your people when you're ready to shoot, it simply means that, the second you're ready to shoot a scene, you announce that you're ready and that you need everyone's attention. Trust me, your cast and crew, if they're at all professional, will immediately put an end to their conversations knowing that they can pick right up where they left off once the scene has been shot. It will be even easier to get everyone's attention if, a couple of weeks before the shoot, you send an email to your entire cast and crew in which you explain to them the need to move quickly on the shoot, and that one of the ways that all of you will be able to move quickly is if conversations are put on an immediate hold when scenes are ready to be shot. Follow this up with an announcement at your rehearsal where you reiterate this thought. With two notices regarding this issue, you should have no problem once you get on set.

When it comes to call times, keep in mind that since you've spread out the call times of your cast members, people will be coming and going throughout the day. This can make for some commotion, especially if you're shooting in tight quarters, but don't let it faze you. You will occasionally need to cut a scene when someone opens a door to enter or leave, or when someone arrives and sees someone they're happy to see and calls out to them. These are not events to get upset about. Simply cut the scene (or if it's going well, keep it going, as you may end up with some good footage that can be edited around) and start over. As the person in charge of the set and the film, the more you keep your composure and a happy countenance, the more it will spill over to everyone on set and allow you to get everything you want to filmed.

Another matter you have to pay constant attention to regards product placement. It is a given that you are not being paid hundreds of thousands of dollars by major corporations to place their products in your film where viewers can see the logos of their products. You might think, however, that it's a good idea to show some products in your film to make it look like you have some product placement deals in place, or you might put out some products with the hope that the company who owns the product will see the film and want to pay you for having done them that favor, or at least work with you in the future, since you gave them some free publicity. This is not the case. In fact, quite the opposite is true. There have been instances where a company did not give a filmmaker the rights to showcase their products in a film, saw their products in the film, and then sued the filmmaker for using their products without permission. So make sure you stay diligent in keeping an eye out for any product logos that might appear in a take and either turn the item around so the logo is hidden or move the item out of frame. And should you miss something while shooting the film and in the edit notice a logo, make sure the editor blurs out the logo or covers it up in some manner before you release your film.

This brings us to one of the most important aspects of being on set—never ever ever yell at anyone. With rare exceptions, everyone working on your film wants to do their best to make the film as good as it can possibly be, so when someone makes a mistake, forgets a line, accidentally interrupts a scene, or whatever, don't make them feel worse than they already feel by calling them out.

There will be some people who are part of your cast and crew who aren't professional or prepared. Is it okay to yell at these people? Certainly not. When a crew member makes a habit of showing up late or not following directions, simply don't bring that crew member back for your next project. When a cast member is routinely late or has to leave early or arrives on set and doesn't know their lines (the absolute minimum every cast member needs to hold themselves accountable for is to arrive on set on time knowing their lines—not having their lines memorized sabotages the entire shoot by grinding it to a halt and is completely disrespectful to everyone on the cast and crew), work around it as best you can. This might mean shooting some extra close-ups or cutaways so you can simply have the cast member read their lines right into the microphone (so you can edit around their failure to know their lines). Then, simply don't bring that actor or actress back to be in any of your future projects. Yelling at someone in situations like this does nothing to improve their performance, and it puts everyone on edge, so never yell at anyone, no matter how frustrating their actions or lack of professionalism might be.

Directing

While you should try to do much of your directing during the rehearsal, there will be plenty of times during the shoot when you have to direct a cast member. Most of the time this will simply consist of telling the actor or actress to do the line or scene again and to do it in a little different manner, the manner which you think will work best. Most actors and actresses have absolutely no problem at all with this and will quickly follow your direction. If by chance you have a particular actor or actress who is really struggling with their performance, find a moment when you can take them off to the side and do your directing one on one. You never want a cast member to feel like you're making them look bad in front of their peers, and a minute or two off to the side politely letting them know what you're looking for can work wonders.

One thing to take notice of when directing your cast is to keep a special eye out for those people in your cast who have done a lot of theater work. Since theater actors really have to project their voice so the people in the last row can hear them, and since they sometimes have to be extra animated on stage so those people in the last row can tell exactly what they're doing, you will sometimes find that theater actors might be a little over the top with their screen performance. If you notice this from one of your cast members, take them off to the side early in the shoot to address the issue so that their performance is not uneven. Should this cast member have been on set first thing in the morning and you timidly wait until the afternoon to say anything as you hope to see them eventually settle into their role, you will end up with an uneven performance from them that finds them being animated in some scenes and reserved in others. This might be okay if you're shooting a spoof comedy, but it might look awful if you're shooting a drama, and since you don't have a big budget to work with, and since you're shooting on a tight schedule, you probably won't be able to afford to go back and reshoot scenes from earlier in the day where you weren't happy with their performance.

Keep in mind that you don't need to be shy or intimidated about directing your cast, even if it's your first film, and even if the cast member you need to speak with is a veteran with lots of film and/or theater experience. The actor will usually appreciate your input, because the last thing he or she wants to see is 80 minutes of movie with them delivering an uneven, poor performance.

This isn't to say that you shouldn't cast people in your films who have an extensive theater background. I have had much success with casting theater people in my films. Actors like Ben Whitehair, Ryan Robins, Jason W. Griffith, and Andrea Rabold have done outstanding jobs in my films in spite of (or maybe because of) their theater experiences. And one of the nice bonuses of using actors with a theater background is that they are typically very good with having their lines memorized, which is a real bonus when filming quickly.

Keep in mind that when you're directing your film, you need to keep it simple—there's no time for trying to act like Stanley Kubrick when you're shooting your film in one or two weekends. You more want to take the approach that John Carpenter took in the making of *Halloween*. Carpenter worked with a lot of young, sometimes inexperienced, cast members in *Halloween*, so he had to keep it simple when directing them. For example, when one of the cast members began to ask him questions about how they should act out a particular scene, Carpenter merely told them to find their mark and say their line. It worked out great. When a scene came up where the character Michael Myers had to walk across the street and the actor playing him asked Carpenter how he should walk and what his motivation was for how he would walk, Carpenter simply told him, "Just walk across the street." Again, it worked out great. Keep the directing simple, and let your script do your work for you.

Wearing Many Hats

Shoot days will be chaos for you—that's just a given. In all likelihood you're director, producer, caterer, wardrobe supervisor, fire-putter-outer, set decorator, advisor, and possibly actor, so you will have people asking questions of you and coming to you with problems all day long. As the captain of the ship, you need to address all of these issues with your full attention and with courteousness.

The range of questions and concerns that will arise is massive. You will get the standard questions of which scene will be shot next, how you want the lighting for the scene, where you want the camera set up, and what blocking do you want for the next scene. While addressing these questions you will also get questions regarding where the bathroom is, whether there are any more cookies left, whether a different blouse might look better on an actress in the upcoming scene, whether an end table can be moved to open up a little room on the set, whether an item in the background needs to be turned a little bit so the logo on it doesn't show, and a hundred other questions throughout the day. Expect this! Every member of the cast and crew is looking to you as their leader, and the way you handle all these questions will set the tone for the entire shoot and will establish how all the people working on your project view you. If you maintain your composure and answer all the questions with a smile on your face, your cast and crew will know you are the captain of the ship.

Keep in mind as well that sometimes you will be asked questions by an actor or crew member that seem to be completely stupid, and that might make you want to derisively shake your head or roll your eyes. Do not do this. The question is obviously important to the person asking it, and no matter how annoying or stupid the question might seem to you, make sure you answer it with respect.

Be Spontaneous

As the shoot progresses, most of the time you will be working hard on simply getting all the shots you need (sometimes you will simply shoot a single master shot of a scene, it'll look good to your naked eye, you'll ask your DP if it looked good to him, he'll say yes, and you'll move on to the next scene), but you need to be open to occasionally changing things up if that will allow you to get a shot that will make your film better. This most often takes the form of adding a little something in, getting a shot from another angle, or changing some dialogue a little bit.

An example of this occurred in *To Die is Hard*. Very late in the shoot we had gotten to the point where we were ready to shoot the climactic fight scene between Joe McCann and the lead terrorist, Anton. Actor Baird Lefter was playing Anton, and we had blocked out much of the fight, but as Joe and Anton finally reached the catwalk for the end of the fight, we wondered if we might do something a little different besides having Joe and Anton punch each other. At this point Baird mentioned that he could do a not-quite-perfect slide kick maneuver, and he demonstrated it for us—it was hilarious. So we told him to just start doing slide kicks, so he did. Over and over and over again. It was a riot! That entire part of the fight consisted of Baird doing 17 slide kicks while throwing just one punch. It completely worked, and it was completely spontaneous.

There are more subtle things that might arise to improve your film. In *The Worst Movie EVER!* there was a subtle change to one line that I made as I was playing Dr. Lars Coolman. As I shot the scene with Kasha Fauscett and Christopher Irvin, it suddenly occurred to me that a slight change to one small line would be a little bit funnier. We shot the scene with the original line, which was, "We've studied robot aliens, ma'am. He'll be back." Then I told the DP, Erik Lassi, to shoot it one more time, and that I was going to change that one line to, "We've studied robot aliens, ma'am. We're scientists." We took an extra 30 seconds, shot the short scene again, and I used the different line. That change added just a little bit more swagger and false bravado to Dr. Coolman, which was a nice contrast to his geekiness. When the film went to the edit, editor Alan Dague-Greene used the improvised line to get an extra giggle in the film.

Keep in mind that you can't afford to reshoot a whole bunch of scenes since you are moving so quickly. However, if you see the chance to add an extra laugh to your film or a little extra tension, and it'll only take a minute or two to do so, go ahead and get that shot. The way I look at it is, at least when it comes to a comedy, every extra laugh or giggle I can get into the film will make it that much more enjoyable for the viewer, which will increase our chances of getting a theatrical or DVD or foreign release for the film. And if you're shooting a horror film or a drama, every little extra bit of tension you add to the film will go a long way toward making your film better and toward giving you the best chance possible of getting a release for your film.

As the Day Moves On

As the day moves from the morning into the afternoon, and as you wear the dozen or so hats that you will inevitably end up wearing, you will begin to get tired. Make sure to keep eating, and drink lots of water so you don't get too dehydrated. You can't allow yourself, though, to focus on how tired you might be getting. There are a lot of people depending on you to get the job done, and you can't let down at any point—there will be time to rest later.

One thing to pay extra attention to at this point in the day is to make sure you don't miss any scenes you need to shoot, and make sure you don't let any cast members leave until you're 100% sure you've shot every scene they are scheduled to be in for the day. Should you miss a scene during the day, it could completely mess up your shoot, especially if the location of that scene is 50 miles away and there are seven or eight people in the scene. Should you miss that one scene, you now have to try to get 10 or so cast and crew members together on an extra day of shooting to pick up a scene that might only take 15 minutes to shoot. When you're paying people a pittance to work on your film, it's not fair to ask them to come in for an extra day. And considering that probably all people involved in the making of your film will have jobs and might not be able to easily get time off, it might take weeks before you're able to get all these people together again to get this one scene shot.

You can also run into serious problems if you fail to notice that a cast member has one more scene that's scheduled to be shot later in the day, and you accidentally let that cast member go home. This actually happened to me during the filming of *The Worst Movie EVER!* Stuart Goldstein had been on set for five hours or so, and he asked me if he could leave since he thought he was done for the day. I checked my scene/cast list for the day and saw he wasn't in any more scenes, so I sent Stuie on his way. An hour later, I realized that he was actually in a few more scenes. Oops. Luckily, Stuie's character, Bobby, was dead during the scenes we needed to shoot, and Stuie only needed to lie dead on the ground as people ran past him. In the edit we were able to cut and paste an earlier shot of him lying dead on the sidewalk into these scenes. It looks awful and tacky, but, hey, it's the worst movie ever, so it worked out great.

However, a simple oversight like that would typically be a major pain in the butt for half a dozen or more people as they would have to come back to shoot the scene at a later date. So when it comes to making sure you have every scene shot that you need to get, and every cast member on set that you'll need, even though the day might be getting long, check, double check, and triple check these things so you don't make a grievous mistake that inconveniences many people.

Summary

As the director, you are the captain of the ship, so make sure you maintain your composure at all times, as this will certainly rub off on your cast and crew. Make sure you are thorough in getting every shot you planned for the day, or you will be faced with the unfortunate and extremely inconvenient task of adding another shoot day to your schedule.

CHAPTER 5

Postproduction

Once the film is shot, if you're not editing the film yourself, you have to relinquish some control over your project. This is not to say that you let your editor do whatever they want with your film, but you have to be able to trust them to a large extent.

When discussing the editing process, you must know that the editor of the film absolutely can make or break your film. On two different projects I've had two different editors edit the film, and on both occasions, the two separate finished versions of the films were almost unbelievably different from each other.

The best example I can give of how important the editor is to the film pertains to the psychological thriller feature film we made titled *Evil Intent*. We shot the film in the summer of 2007. On the advice of one of the cast members, I gave the footage to a friend of his who, he said, was a great editor. I checked out one of her short films to verify this, and it was quite good. So I gave her the footage.

Nearly a year later, after having checked in with her many times to make sure things were going okay, she finally admitted that she had barely even started on the edit, so I got the footage from her and gave it to a guy who had edited a short film for me previously. Two years later, this guy delivered the film to me, and it was awful. The film verged on being painful to watch. I figured it came down to the fact that we had simply made an awful film (which really confused me, since DP Gene Yanza had gotten so many great shots and the cast gave such a tremendous performance), and I figured I'd give a copy to all the people involved in the film and never let the film see the light of day. However, my girlfriend Diane Henry asked if she could watch it, so I said okay. (Diane has played an extra in two of our films and helped out with catering, handling the boom mic, wardrobe, etc., on multiple projects of ours—what a great way to cut costs on a shoot: have your girlfriend do cast and crew things for free!) She and I watched it together, and when it finished, she looked at me and said, "Wow, that was really good, but the editing sucked." As I picked her brain, she said she loved the plot, and she loved the performances in the film, but the editing was just so awful as to make the film hard to follow at times.

With her input, I then got the footage to another guy I had worked with previously, Brian Cabrera, and told him I would give him a month to do an edit on the film. A month later he delivered to me a completely different film that I was thrilled with. With the first edit of the film, on a scale of zero to four stars, I would have given the film half a star. With Brian's new edit, I give the film two and a half stars. Brian used the exact same footage but came up with a completely different product.

I can't stress to you the importance of having a good editor. A good editor means more to the film than anything besides the script, and that's why I give more money to my editors than any other person in the cast or crew. If I have a film with a budget of $1500, I will give the editor at least $500 of that budget, if not even upwards of $750.

It's also important to find an editor who will actually work hard to get the film completed. As you can see with *Evil Intent*, editors can frequently put your project aside for lengthy periods of time, and rest assured, they won't tell you this. You can check in on them, and they will say they're working on it, but there's a good chance they're not working on it, or, if they are, they are working very slowly on it. There might be legitimate reasons for them to have your film on the back burner—many editors are working full-time jobs, they're working on other films, they're working on their own films, and they might have families to tend to. Or if they're younger, they might have frequent parties to attend. And since you're only giving them a matter of hundreds of dollars to edit your film, the per-hour rate they're getting for the job isn't enough to make them throw themselves into the editing process.

You can also see from my *Evil Intent* experience that an excellent job can be done on a feature film in just a month's time. Thankfully, Brian had plenty of time at his disposal when he edited *Evil Intent*, and he used that time to do a great job on the film.

Also, make sure that you don't pay your editors everything up front. Give them a few hundred dollars to get them going, and tell them they'll get the rest when the film is completed. I have lost quite a bit of money in paying editors up front only to have them do little to nothing with the footage (or a god-awful job with it), and, believe you me, they never offer to give any of the money back for a job poorly, or not at all, done.

One of the ways to help protect yourself from getting burned by an editor is to periodically ask to see the footage they have edited together. Don't be afraid to ask for changes because, after all, it is your film. This is one of the areas where I really failed in the first edit of *Evil Intent*. The editor would get me some footage he had worked on, I'd watch it, I'd get back to him about changes I wanted made, and then when I saw his reedit of the scenes a couple months later, much of what I had asked for he hadn't changed. I assumed he just didn't have the footage to work with to make the changes (even though I knew we had shot the footage that was needed to make the changes in the edit I asked for, I convinced myself that that footage must not have been usable), only to find out that when Brian did the reedit, the footage was most certainly there. I should have been firmer and demanded the editor put the time into the changes or else taken all the raw footage back on the spot and gotten it into the hands of someone else. The thought process I fell prey to was telling myself that the editor had already had the material for well over a year after someone else had sat on it for a year, and that I just needed to get a finished version at some point, and that getting the footage to yet another editor might add another year or two to the process.

Keep in mind that there is at least one other good reason why you would want to change the editor of your film, and this happened to me with *Therapissed*. I had been introduced to an editor through a mutual friend, and after talking with this guy and seeing some of his work, I brought him on to edit *Therapissed*. A couple of weeks after I dropped off the footage with him, I gave him a call and asked how the edit was coming along. This editor informed me that he really hadn't edited anything yet because in downloading the footage, he didn't think it was very good. I immediately went over to his house and grabbed the footage from him because there was no way I was going to let a guy edit a film of mine if he didn't think it was very good, as that's a sure recipe for a half-hearted editing effort that completely ruins the film.

If you're fortunate enough to find a talented editor who will diligently work at getting your film completed (there's no reason for a film to take more than eight or nine months to edit, and a hard-working editor can certainly finish the job in one to four months), use that editor as often as possible in your future projects. A good editor is truly hard to find.

At this point you might be wondering why you shouldn't edit your film yourself. If you know how to edit and have a good editing program on your computer, this is certainly an option for you. And it is also an option to take a month or two to completely immerse yourself in learning how to edit so you can edit your own projects down the road. If this sounds enticing to you, by all means do it. I have not gone this route, however, for two main reasons.

The primary reason I don't edit my own films is that editing is a major consumer of time. While editing is at times a thrilling, exciting venture, much of the editing process consists of doing tedious work that can drag on for weeks. This is time I would rather be spending working on my next script or shooting my next film. Editing your own projects can take you from being able to make one or two feature films a year to making one film every year and a half or so, and simple math will tell you that if over the course of four years you make six features, you are two times more likely to break through as a filmmaker than if over the course of those four years you make three films.

Another reason I don't edit my own films is that an editor with an outside point of view can often bring some real insights to the film that I had never even contemplated. A great example of this is my frequent collaborator Alan Dague-Greene. Alan has an incredibly insightful mind, and he will add wonderful little touches to scenes that I would have never done, let alone considered. One of my favorite examples of this is with *To Die is Hard*. Late in the movie when the climactic fight scene between Joe McCann and Anton is taking place, we made the mistake of not noticing there was a Pepsi vending machine in the background. Now, most editors would have simply covered over the Pepsi logo so the vending machine was nothing more than a big blue rectangle in the background, and no one would have even noticed. But Alan is much more creative than that.

What Alan proceeded to do was take a picture of himself with a really happy, excited look on his face, trace around his face (leaving off his neck) so it was one of those floating head things, paste his head over the Pepsi logo, and then splash a "Humpty Broth" logo across the vending machine. It's priceless! And while most people don't even notice the vending machine because it's far off to the side while viewers' eyes are focused on Joe and Anton fighting, and because it's only up on screen for maybe one second, it is a wonderful, hilarious addition to the film that I would never have thought of doing. I mean, seriously—why would any company name themselves Humpty Broth, and why would said company think it's a good idea to sell their broths in vending machines? Classic!

So while there are plusses and minuses to doing the editing yourself, if you have a trusted editor you can turn the project over to, I highly suggest you do that while you busily get to work on making your next film.

One other aspect to keep an eye on for your film is to make sure your editor makes the film at least 70 minutes long to improve your chances of getting a release for the film. While you might think this means padding the film with unnecessary footage that could kill the pacing of your film, keep in mind that you can easily add an extra minute or two into the closing credits to get your film up to that magic 70-minute mark, or up to the even more magical 80-minute mark, if your film is close to being that long. Here's why and how you can go about adding time into your closing credits.

The reason you can lengthen your closing credits is twofold. First, most people stop watching the film when the credits begin rolling, so whether your closing credits are two minutes long or 15 minutes long is pretty much irrelevant to most viewers. The second reason you can lengthen your closing credits is because most Hollywood films have anywhere from four to seven minutes of closing credits. This comes into play because, let's face it, with your skeleton crew and small cast, your closing credits could certainly be only 60 to 90 seconds long. But because it's perfectly okay to have four or five minutes of closing credits, you shouldn't feel bad about adding an extra minute or two of them to your film.

So how do you go about lengthening the credits? There are many ways to do this. You can leave each name in the credits up on screen an extra second each. You can add in a lengthy "Thank you" section in the credits with made-up names and businesses. You can make up some crew roles that didn't really exist, and then credit your actual crew members. Finding four or five ways to add an extra 10 or 20 seconds into your closing credits might make your film much more marketable if that extra minute or two takes your film up to the 70- or 80-minute mark. And keep in mind that film length is measured by every full and partial minute of the film. For example, a film that is 79 minutes and 40 seconds long is considered an 80-minute movie. And a film that is 79 minutes and 2 seconds long is also considered to be an 80-minute movie.

When it comes to lengthening your film, you also have the option of shooting some additional scenes. These don't have to be elaborate scenes, and they can really add something positive to your film. For example, when Nick Falls finished the initial edit of *Therapissed*, it was a few minutes shy of 70 minutes. A film of that length has almost no future, so what I did was add in some extra scenes with a new character. Since a huge chunk of the film is made up of showing the psychologist, Dr. Mark Jenkins, in therapy sessions with his various patients, I simply created a new patient, Chet Nussbaum, and I gave that character a handful of therapy session scenes with Dr. Jenkins that were sprinkled in throughout the film. It was quite simple to shoot these new scenes, as the only people on set when we shot them were Greg Nemer (who played Dr. Jenkins), Nick Falls (who was the DP of the film as well as the editor), and me (since I played the role of Chet). We shot the scenes in my apartment. Nick mounted the microphone on a stand so we didn't need a sound guy, we shot the scenes in about an hour's time, and, as it turned out, the Chet character ended up being many viewers' favorite character in the film. So not only did we add seven or eight minutes into the film, we made the film more entertaining as well.

Music

One expense that filmmakers often run up against is purchasing the rights to use certain music in their films. This is a completely unnecessary expense.

To start with, there are plenty of Internet websites out there where you can purchase fantastic music for your film, and lots of it, for little money, often no more than $100 (some websites even have free music for downloading). And if you don't want to invest that much into your film, you can

probably find some local bands who will allow you to use
their music for nothing as they're simply happy to get their
music out there and be able to say that their songs appeared
on the soundtrack of a feature film.

Another option for your film is to find someone who will
independently compose music for your film for free or at a
small price. Just like with local bands, there are thousands
of incredibly talented musicians out there who know how
to use a keyboard and their computer, can compose some
fantastic material for your film, and will be happy to see
their name in the credits and hope to be able to use the
exposure to advance their career. Place an ad on some Internet sites looking for a composer who will work for free or
a few bucks, and you're almost assured of getting multiple
responses to your ad.

I've been extremely lucky when it comes to music in
my films as I can play the guitar, and my frequent editor/
DP Alan Dague-Greene is an excellent musician and music
producer, so we've formed the band Norwegian Soft Kit-
ten. NSK has performed the theme songs for both *To Die
is Hard* and *The Worst Movie EVER!* as well as most of the
other music for those films. While composing the music for
our films certainly adds a little more work to the making of
the film, nothing could be more affordable. The previous
bands I was in with my brother Brian Berggoetz, Please Respond and Fruit Bowl, put together a couple demo tapes,

and we've used the songs from those demo tapes in many of my earlier films. Again, very affordable.

But what if you have to have one particular song for your film? What if there's that one perfect song out there that was a big hit in the '80s or '90s that is so perfect for a particularly important scene in your film that if you can't get it, your film just won't work? If that's the case, then you have a lousy script and film. If the success of your film is dependent upon having to have one particular song that perfectly captures the essence of a scene or your film, then you have a poor film. There are so many appropriate songs out there that will fit the mood of your film, and trying to come up with $10,000 or $25,000 or even much more to get the rights to a well-known song is ludicrous. I've read on multiple occasions about independent filmmakers (who had much more than $2000 in their budget) who thought they absolutely had to have a particular song in their film, only to find out that the cost to get that song was way out of their price range. So what happened? They had to settle for another song they thought was vastly inferior to the original song, only to realize that the song they could afford worked perfectly. So don't get wed to a particular song or band or musician who you think you have to have for your film, because there are many songs and performers that will work just as well.

Summary

The success of your film depends upon you finding a good editor who will work quickly to get your film done. More so than anyone else involved in your film, splurge a little financially to make sure you have a top-notch editor handling the footage you worked so hard to get.

CHAPTER 6

Getting Your Film Released

When it comes to getting a distributor to take on your film, you have to keep two very important things in mind. One, you have to be your film's biggest fan, and two, no matter how many times you might be told "no," it only takes one "yes" to possibly change your life.

While there are multiple ways to get your film out there, your best chance is to land a distributor for your film who loves it as much as you do, who will take on the distribution rights of your film for two to five years. (Don't sign away your rights for any longer than five years, because if things are going well with the company, they'll want to sign another deal with you to retain the rights when the contract is up, and if things aren't going well, you'll want to get a different distributor to handle your film.) Distributors do different things. Some focus solely on trying to get DVD releases for the films in their catalogues. Others focus on video on demand (VOD) releases or foreign sales. Some look for TV deals. Some try for theatrical releases. Some focus on the Internet. Some do all of these.

What I did to find a distributor was to sign up on the IMDb website for their gold service so I could have access to the contact information of just about everyone in the world with ties to the film and television industry. It costs a little over $100 a year for this access, but it's certainly worth it to independent filmmakers.

I took a lot of time and trolled through the section on distributors and tried to find those who seemed like they would be the most willing to take a look at the first feature film I completed, *Therapissed*. I found a few dozen who seemed like they might be a good fit and contacted them, some with actual letters, others via email. (I haven't seen an appreciable difference in response percentage based upon snail mail versus email, so don't be afraid to use email to make contacts—this will also save you a bunch of money on postage and envelopes.) A handful of these dozens of distribution companies agreed to take a look at the film, a few showed interest, and I eventually chose one to go with.

Keep in mind that when you begin to contact distributors, studios, agents, and production companies, whether you contact them with a letter or an email, the vast majority of them will never even acknowledge that you contacted them. Of those who do acknowledge your inquiry, nearly all of them will reply with a quick "no thanks." When it comes to those who do listen to your inquiry and ask you to send in a copy of your film, most of them will never acknowledge that you sent them a DVD or whether they liked it or not. This is a pretty good sign they're not interested in your film, but still, always follow up with these people just in case it's something else, like they misplaced the DVD you sent them. Of those who do respond to your film, nearly all will say no, whether it's because they didn't like the film or it doesn't quite fit their catalog or they're not taking on any films at the time or whatever. However, if you're lucky, one or two will like your film enough to get back in touch with you. Even then, that's still not a guarantee they will offer you a deal, as they might just want to learn more about you or the film and may still end up passing on it.

What it comes down to is that, in all likelihood, you will have to endure hundreds and hundreds of nos for each yes you get. Don't let this deter you. This does not mean your film is no good—all it means is that the competition out there is really tough, and there are a lot of people making films, and you just have to find the right person in the right position to say yes. You might have to endure a million nos, but if you get that one right person to say yes just one time, you may end up spending the rest of your life being able to make films for a living.

One note with distribution companies: never, ever, ever go with a distributor who charges you a fee up front to represent your film. I did this against my better judgment one time, and after months and months of them failing to respond to a single inquiry I made to them, I (luckily) was able to get out of the contract. Did they return any of my money, even though they didn't make a single sale? No. I've heard plenty of horror stories about distributors like this, so don't make the same mistake I made.

Regardless of how many times you might get rejected with your film, you have to remain your film's biggest fan. If you give up on it and stop trying to get it out there, your film will die, and there's not much point in making a film if no one sees it. Yes, it is fun and exhilarating to make a film, but people make films because they have something to say, because they want to entertain others and provoke people and make people think and laugh. If you stop championing your film, no one else is going to do it for you, and whatever dreams you had for that film will simply fade away.

There are more ways than one, however, to get your film out there. Of course, all of us are aware of the film festival route to gain attention for your film and try to get a deal. Keep a couple of things in mind, though, when it comes to film festivals. First, unless your film is being shown at a major festival or in a major city, there will probably be no one in attendance who is in a position to launch your career. Yes, it is fun to see your film up on a big screen, and it's great to have people tell you afterwards that they enjoyed it, but neither of these things do anything to get your film a wide release anywhere. So if you're going to submit your film to film festivals, focus on the major festivals, and focus on those festivals that are in Los Angeles and New York where, if you are an official selection of the festival, there's a chance someone (a producer, a buyer, a distributor, a film critic) who might be able to help your career along and get your film out to a wider audience will be in attendance.

Another thing to keep in mind with film festivals is that they can get expensive. If you submit your film to just 20 festivals, that could cost you in the range of $1,000 to $1,500 in entry fees alone, which would be enough money to make your next film. On top of that, if your film gets selected to be screened in a festival, you'll probably want to attend the festival, and if you do that, you could be set back another $500 or more to travel to the festival and get a hotel room for a few nights. So assuming you decide to get aggressive with your film and you send it out to 30 festivals and get selected for two of them, and attend both screenings, you could end up dishing out in the range of $3,000. That might be money better spent in other ways.

On occasion, though, there can be some fantastic benefits to having your film screened at a film festival, even if it's not a festival being held in New York or LA. For example, you might meet someone at a festival who can have a major positive impact on your film career. When our film *To Die is Hard* won a Golden Ace Award at the Las Vegas International Film Festival in the summer of 2010, I met film critic

Terra King at the festival. Terra ended up loving *To Die is Hard* and gave the film a great review, which helped to get the word out. Later, she also gave our film *The Worst Movie EVER!* a great review (and picked it as one of the 10 best independent feature films of 2011), which certainly helped to bring plenty of attention to the film and helped us to land some deals.

Another benefit of going the film festival route is that sometimes you meet great people at them and have a great time. *The Worst Movie EVER!* made its film festival debut at the 2011 Van Wert (OH) Independent Film Festival (now known as the Northwest Ohio Independent Film Festival). During the few days I spent in Van Wert at the festival, I struck up an enduring friendship with festival director Len Archibald; I met film producer Theodore James, who gave me the contact information for Myles Shane and Hiltz Squared Media (who ended up taking on the worldwide distribution rights to *The Worst Movie EVER!*); and I got to experience many laughs with Kirk Dougal, Christopher Butturff, Joe Maurer, Jonathan Hodges, Linda McClure, Sally Geething, Jessica Archibald, Dave Mosier, and many other incredible people who are part of that wonderful festival.

Of course, I've had experiences at other festivals where I talked with a few people, attended a couple of events tied in with the festival, and watched my film, and that was the extent of it. No lasting friendships, no contacts with critics or producers, and no particularly memorable times.

As you can see, the film festival route can vary from one extreme to the other, so it's a gamble submitting your film to festivals. My suggestion is to research the festivals you're considering submitting your film to, pick the four or five that seem the most promising to you based upon what you want out of a festival (overcoming the odds to try to get exposure at a major festival, being a big fish in a smaller pond for a couple days, making friendships, networking with other filmmakers, etc.), and then submit to those festivals.

Another route you have for getting your film out there is to contact independent theaters on your own about showing your film. On my own I was able to track down nearly 100 truly independent theaters around the US, and I contacted all of them regarding my film *To Die is Hard*. (Keep in mind that many so-called independent theaters are actually owned by national chains and only show those independent films that are released by the subsidiaries of major studios or through major distribution companies and had budgets in the $4 million to $8 million range and have one to three well-known stars in them, so they won't even consider responding to your inquiries, let alone actually watch your film to see if it's any good. Those $6 million films from the big studios' subsidiaries don't seem very independent to me, but what do I know.) While the vast majority of these theaters never even acknowledged my inquiries (I contacted all of them multiple times), nearly 30 of the theaters requested a DVD of the film, and through persistence and follow-up emails, I was able to get three of them to agree to show the film. While a few screenings in a few independent theaters will hardly be enough to allow me to retire, this can turn out to be the foot in the door that helps my future films to get wider theatrical releases, and the limited release will make it a bit easier for my distributor to find foreign, VOD, and DVD deals for the film. I've had even better luck with my film *The Worst Movie EVER!* In contacting independent theaters, I've been able to get the film into seven different theaters, and the film is still making the theatrical rounds. Once again, you can't let a whole lot of nos keep you from pushing your film and getting it out to a wider audience.

When contacting theaters, distributors, studios, agents, production companies, or anyone regarding your film, make sure you are always polite and professional. With the preponderance of inquiries that nearly all of these businesses get on a weekly basis regarding hundreds of films, the absolute minimum you can do for your film is to present yourself as a professional. A sloppily written email or letter with spelling errors and punctuation mistakes will mark you as an amateur and give the reader of the email or letter a quick excuse to click on the delete button or wad your letter up and pitch it into the recycle bin.

One major thing you need to always keep in mind as a filmmaker is that every single day you need to take at least one step forward in keeping your career on the path you want it to take. Often this takes the form of contacting at least one distributor, studio, theater, agent, or producer a day. Sometimes it might mean contacting 20 or 30 or more of these people in a day. Sometimes it might mean spending some time working on a script or checking in with an editor to make sure things are coming along okay. Sometimes it might mean jotting down some ideas you have for a future script. Sometimes it might mean proofreading a script and making minor revisions. Just make sure that every single day you do at least one thing to keep your career moving forward.

When it comes to getting your film out there, be open to all kinds of routes you can take. While it's great to get a distributor for your film who will handle selling the film to various markets, if you don't land a distributor, there are other ways to get your film seen. There are multiple Internet companies out there who take on indie films, and every time someone downloads your film, you make a little money. While this process will probably not make you rich, at least it makes you a little something, and even better, you now have a chance that someone in a position to give your career a boost might stumble across your film. Yes, I realize there are tens of thousands of films out there, and the odds of a studio executive or agent or producer coming across your film and loving it are slim. But at least there's a chance, which you certainly wouldn't have if you never made your film in the first place or pushed to get it released after you finished it.

One thing to keep in mind is that if you are fortunate enough to land a distributor for your film, that doesn't mean you have it made. There are hundreds of distribution companies out there who are all pushing dozens, if not hundreds, of films each, so even with a distribution company on your side, the competition is still exceedingly fierce in trying to get your film released. Landing a distribution deal isn't your ticket to take 12 months off and lollygag around as you wait for the big bucks to start rolling in. It's merely confirmation that you know what you're doing when it comes to making films and that you need to keep making more of them.

Make sure to keep in mind that you owe it to your cast and crew members to do everything you can to get your film sold. These people put a lot of effort in helping you make your film, and you paid them very little, so the least you can do for them is bust your hump in trying to get the film sold somewhere. And if you do get the film released, it may turn out to be one of your cast members' big break, as their performance may get noticed by a critic or producer or agent who can launch their career.

Another fun thing you can do for your cast and crew is to rent a theater to screen the film once the final edit is in place. If you look hard enough, you should be able to find a decent theater you can rent for $300 to $500. If you charge people $5 each to get in, even a minimal crowd of the cast and crew and some of their friends and family members should allow you to break even for the night, and everyone will have a good time as they get to see themselves or their work up on a big screen. And who knows, if you spread the word around about the screening and get your cast and crew to bring lots of friends and family members, you might end up with 150 people in the theater and an extra couple of hundred dollars in your pocket to put toward making your next film. Make sure that when you hold this screening that you allow your cast and crew members to attend for free, and also make sure you give each of them a free DVD of the film.

So what happens if no one wants your film? No distributor wants to add it to their catalog, no studio wants to look at it, no independent theater owner wants to show it, no Internet website wants to make it available for download. What do you do if you can't get anyone to take a chance on your film? You make another film! One unsold film does not mean the end of your dreams.

Did you notice that I didn't say "one failed film" in the previous sentence? That's because even if you made an awful film (and that happens to the best of us), you will still have hopefully learned more than you could have imagined by making it, and you will be able to carry this knowledge over to your next project. With this new knowledge you will not only be able to avoid some of the mistakes you may have made in making your previous film, but you will have learned something about what makes a film funnier or more dramatic or scarier. And while it might seem logical to sit around and wallow in misery over your unsold film, there is no time for wallowing when you're an independent filmmaker—you have to keep creating, you have to keep writing, you have to keep directing, you have to keep making your films!

One of the most important things that might come from having made your unsold film is that you may have crossed paths with some seriously talented actors and actresses who, since you treated them with respect and dignity during the making of the unsold film, will be happy to work with you again, which might make your next film much better than your previous film. And you never know—some day one of these seriously talented people may get their break in Hollywood and become a well-known star, and then you'll almost certainly be able to sell your previously unsold film with them in it, even if it's five or 10 years old by then.

So keep pushing your film. Yes, the odds are against you getting a deal for it, but you never know when something might fall your way.

Your Next Film

On many occasions I have heard stories of this happening to filmmakers: they make their film, it breaks through

GETTING YOUR FILM RELEASED

somewhere and gets some notice, the filmmaker gets an audience with some producers and studio execs who liked the film, the execs ask the filmmaker what scripts they have ready for shooting their next film, the filmmaker admits to not having any other scripts written, and then the film-maker is ushered out of the meeting and never hears from the producers and execs again.

While your film is being edited, and while you're busy trying to sell your film once it's completed, you absolutely must be working on your next script in case you do get that audience with producers and studio executives. If, during that meeting, you're able to enthusiastically tell those people about a script you have, you might walk out of that meet-ing with a deal in place. Better yet, walk into that meeting with multiple scripts ready to go to improve your chances of getting a deal. Remember, you don't have to take a year or two to write a script; take a week or two, or a month or two (as a side note, this book took me seven days to write from start to finish, and with a thorough rewrite). Then write your next one. If you want, go ahead and write that script that would take $20 million to shoot and save it for when you do get that meeting.

And don't be afraid to explore other genres outside your comfort zone. I primarily write and make comedies, but of the 14 completed feature film scripts I have ready to put into production should I be able to land a big deal, I have a couple of dramas, a horror film, and a chick flick. At the very minimum, by writing these other scripts, I've become a better writer by forcing myself to approach scripts with a different mindset and by exploring different ways to go about character and plot development. And should I get that meeting with some studio heads, and should they want to work with me, but only if I have a dramatic script to shoot, then I'll be ready for them.

As an independent filmmaker, you have to try to make sure you're ready for just about anything that comes your way, especially if it's an opportunity to make a film with studio backing. Don't disappoint yourself and miss what may be your big chance simply because you didn't work hard enough.

CHAPTER 7

Checklist

Let's list each step of the filmmaking process so you can see exactly what you have to do to get your film made in one easy-to-read list.

1. Write your script: limit the characters and locations.
2. Find your money: this frequently means simplifying your spending habits.
3. Put your cast and crew together.
4. Line up your locations: use locations that don't require permits or fees.
5. Hold a rehearsal.
6. Make sure everything is ready for the shoot: food, props, clothes, etc.
7. Shoot the film.
8. Edit the film.
9. Contact distributors, studios, theaters, producers, agents, etc.
10. Write your next script or two.

As you go through these steps, make sure you enjoy the process of making your film. It's quite easy to get stressed out and to be filled with worry as you make your film and attend to all the details that come with making a film, but remember that you are not making films to be famous (though that could be a very nice perk should you do a good job and someone notices that), you are making films because you love making them—you love writing a fantastic script, you love working with talented people, you love being able to be creative and create something new, you love the thrill of finally seeing your finished product and sharing it with others. So make sure that when you have those moments or days when it all seems a bit overwhelming, when you have those times when nothing seems to go right and you're feeling frustrated, that you take a step back, take a deep breath, and realize what a truly incredible experience it is to work on a film, to be a filmmaker. It's not the final destination that matters, it's the journey, the process that matters. And along the course of that journey, you will have many unbelievable, hilarious experiences that you will remember for the rest of your life.

Always remember as well that making a film is not brain surgery, that you don't have to make it harder than it needs to be. Yes, there are 250 big and little things you need to take care of to make your film, but there are also a lot of myths going around out there about things people say you need to do to make your film but that you really don't need to concern yourself with. Keep your script simple, keep your crew simple, and get your film shot in a couple of weeks, not a couple of years. You are not making a film that will win an Academy Award for best picture or best director or best screenplay or best costumes or best actress or best supporting actor. You are making a film that will entertain people, that will make people laugh, that will scare people, that will make people cry, and that will hopefully be good enough to catch enough people's eyes so that, for your next film, someone will give you more money to work with than you know what to do with.

Index